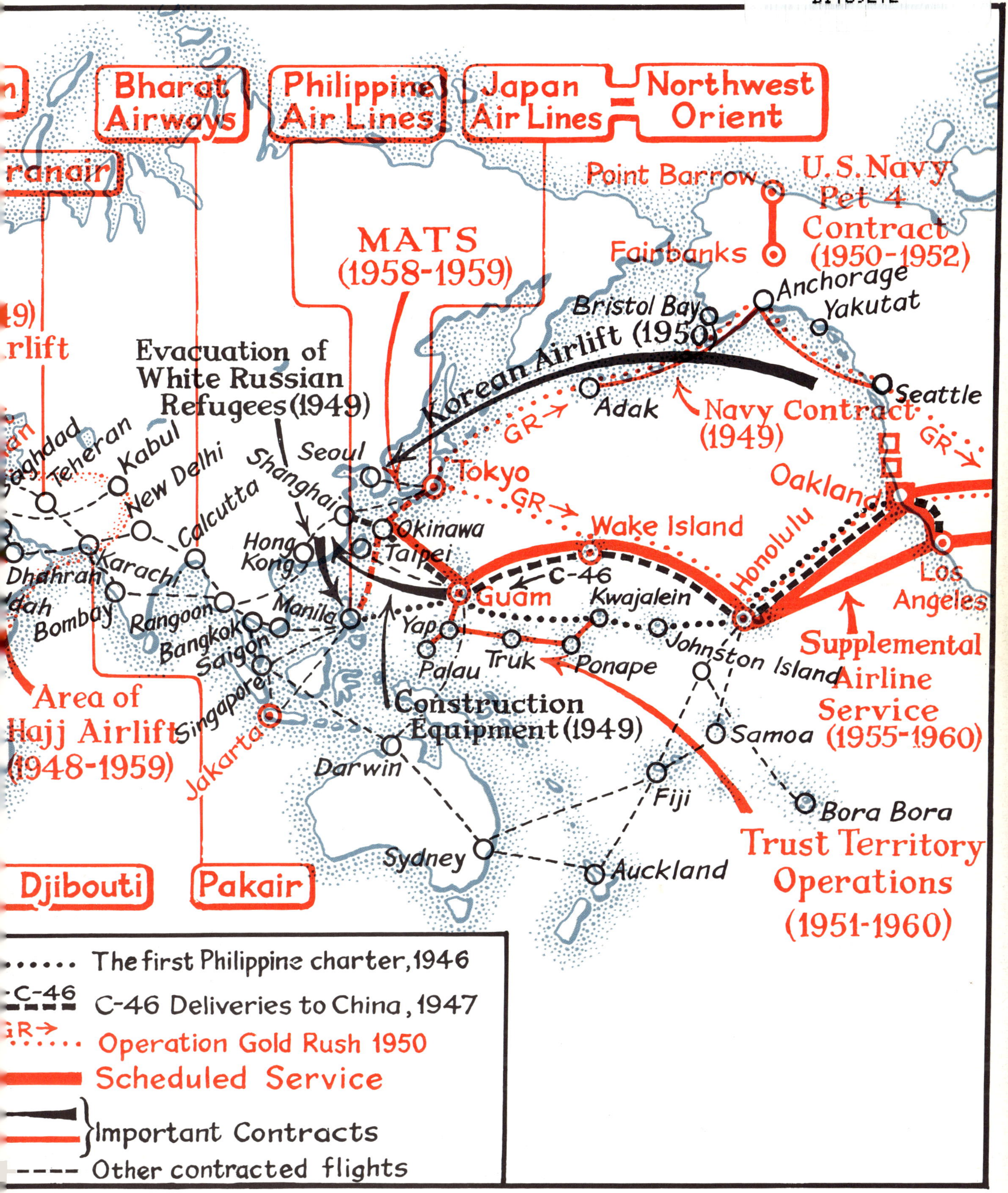
Bharat Airways
Philippine Air Lines
Japan Air Lines
Northwest Orient
ranair
Point Barrow
U.S. Navy Pet 4 Contract (1950-1952)
Fairbanks
MATS (1958-1959)
Anchorage
Bristol Bay
Yakutat
Korean Airlift (1950)
Evacuation of White Russian Refugees (1949)
Adak
Seattle
Navy Contract (1949)
GR
Seoul
Shanghai
Tokyo
Oakland
Baghdad
Teheran
Kabul
New Delhi
Calcutta
Okinawa
Wake Island
Honolulu
Dhahran
Karachi
Hong Kong
Taipei
C-46
Los Angeles
Bombay
Rangoon
Manila
Guam
Kwajalein
Bangkok
Saigon
Yap
Palau
Truk
Ponape
Johnston Island
Supplemental Airline Service (1955-1960)
Singapore
Jakarta
Construction Equipment (1949)
Area of Hajj Airlift (1948-1959)
Darwin
Samoa
Fiji
Bora Bora
Sydney
Auckland
Trust Territory Operations (1951-1960)
Djibouti
Pakair
The first Philippine charter, 1946
C-46 Deliveries to China, 1947
Operation Gold Rush 1950
Scheduled Service
Important Contracts
Other contracted flights

One of TAL's Stratocruisers, N1027V, parked at John Rogers Airport, Honolulu, Hawaii. Later re-registered by TAL—N401Q. AS

Folded Wings
A History of Transocean Air Lines

by ARUE SZURA

PICTORIAL HISTORIES PUBLISHING COMPANY
Missoula, Montana

COPYRIGHT © 1989 BY ARUE B. SZURA

All rights reserved. No part of this book
may be used or reproduced without
written permission of the publisher.

LIBRARY OF CONGRESS
CATALOG CARD NUMBER 88-90965

ISBN 0-929521-04-8

First Printing: May 1989

PRINTED IN CANADA

Layout: Stan Cohen, Missoula, Montana
Typography: Arrow Graphics, Missoula, Montana

The map on the inside cover of Transocean's operations from its foundation in 1946 until its demise in 1960 provides some idea of the extraordinary flexibility of the organization in tackling almost any mission or accepting any challenge, all in the interests of widening the scope of air transport. Why this airline never received the scheduled operating certificate that it so richly deserved will remain one of the mysteries in the annals of airline history. Its record clearly shows that it was fit, willing, and able—in fact totally qualified.

MAP COURTESY OF R.E.G. DAVIES

PICTORIAL HISTORIES PUBLISHING COMPANY
713 South Third West, Missoula, Montana 59801

Foreword
by R.E.G. Davies

Orvis Nelson was possibly the greatest of all airline promoters who never reaped the just rewards of his enterprise, innovation and determination. During little more than a decade, he built an organization, Transocean Air Lines, that could challenge any other air transport company in any category of commercial aviation. Orvis built up a team of flying crew, ground support staff and administration that set new standards of improvised efficiency because it was backed by a collective resource of experience and versatility that was second to none.

Transocean's influence was world-wide. Quite apart from the dozens of flying contracts involving passenger loads as diverse in character as wartime brides, youthful tourists, Jewish refugees, and Moslem pilgrims, Nelson and his merry men and women helped to establish many a national airline that survives today, provided technical support for countless others, and finally reached the goal of all aspiring air transport fanatics with gasoline in their blood and hydraulic fluid under their fingernails: they started a scheduled airline.

Arue Szura captures the adventure, the romance and the true spirit of pioneering that was the essence of Transocean. She herself would be the first to admit that, comprehensive though it is, as much again could be written as additional delightful anecdotal punctuation to the narrative. But no matter, to the uninitiated, to those whose memories do not go back to the cavalier years of the post-war era, this book should be a lexicon to remind them that the airlines were not built just by the injection of vast sums of capital or by the legislation and the regulation that created the present-day giants of the industry. They were also built by remarkable individuals like Orvis Nelson.

The biggest irony is that Transocean's very success led to its downfall. Vested interests in the airline industry, comfortable under their protected blanket of designated route networks and government subsidy, lobbied insidiously and incessantly to protect what they had come to believe was an inviolate right. The Civil Aeronautics Board, which had ruled the industry as if it were a closed society of privileged aristocrats who could not be allowed to admit lesser mortals into their midst, came to the incumbents' aid with the kind of bureaucratic litigation that defies objective analysis.

When the combined forces of Washington reaction finally won the battle to stop Orvis Nelson from entering the ranks of the scheduled airlines, it was one of the biggest travesties of justice ever perpetrated in the history of air transport. Transocean had been good enough for the U.S. Navy, for the Military Air Transport Service, for the International Refugee Organization, for the United States Trust Territory Administration, for Christians, Jews and Moslems all over the world; but it was not good enough for the C.A.B. and its convoluted protectionism.

By demonstrating its capability of operating scheduled services in Micronesia and later, in one glorious bid for recognition, in operating Boeing Stratocruisers across the Pacific on scheduled, albeit limited frequency, flights — scaring the incumbents half to death — Transocean earned an honored place in history. Orvis Nelson was before his time; for in the era of airline deregulation that was the sequel to the closed-shop environment that dug its own grave, Transocean would not only have participated in the transpacific air routes, it would have dominated them.

I have, therefore, only one reservation about Arue's book, and that is to wonder how she could have been so forgiving toward those whose jealousies brought Orvis to heel at the bitter end. Perhaps it is because, in seeking what the scholars call prime source material, she met the hundreds of men and women who *were* Transocean, and whose memories were inevitably of the great times they had in building something that was worth while, of years spent in creative activity that they can look back to with pride; and of which mere observers like me can only read about with envy.

Arue Szura has concentrated on all the positive aspects of a great airline. She has faithfully recorded the excitement, the joy and the special quality that made up the band of dedicated people whom Orvis Nelson intuitively assembled with such success that the bond still remains today in its Alumni Society. I know that Stan Cohen will do his usual superb job of producing an attractive book. I cannot wait to see it in print.

Introduction

To tell the story of Transocean Air Lines is to live once again the fairy tale of Prince Ahmed and his magic carpet; for Transocean traveled to virtually every corner of the world during its halcyon days from 1946 to 1960.

Unlike the magic carpet of old, however, the men and women of Transocean Air Lines barnstormed around the globe during the 1940s and 1950s in DC-3s, DC-4s, DC-6s, Stratocruisers, Super Constellations, and other aircraft; aviation pioneers in the truest sense of the word.

Transocean flight crews never knew where fortune would take them, or for how long, as contracts were often found along the way. Typical of their life, a crew once left Oakland, California, for Formosa in a DC-4 loaded with twelve thousand pounds of gunpowder for General Chiang Kai-Shek's Nationalist Chinese Army, then ferried the airplane to Hong Kong to pick up a load of Chinese cedar chests and fly them west to Rome, Italy. Within hours of the delivery of the cedar chests, the airplane departed full of Italian seamen bound for New York to rendezvous with an ocean freighter.

Nor was it uncommon for flight crews to leave California in 70 degree weather for the sun-blistered Middle East where temperatures soared to 134 degrees, then fly to Alaska where the mercury plunged to 60 below zero, all in a matter of days.

Millions of dollars in gold bullion were transported aboard Transocean aircraft as well as diverse payloads such as monkeys, coal, bazookas, bees, helicopters, and goats. TAL pilots also flew missions to Shanghai, Germany, and Hungary to rescue hundreds of refugees from communist invaders at a time before radar and other modern flying aids were available.

Organized by a handful of maverick aviators with more dreams than money in their pockets, Transocean Air Lines eventually became the largest supplemental air carrier in the world, employing at its peak over 6,700 workers at some fifty-seven bases around the globe.

More than forty years have passed since the fledgling airline first took to the skies on that morning, March 16, 1946. That began a fourteen year 'round-the-world odyssey filled with the kind of adventures that pilots of today can only dream about.

Transocean Air Lines folded its wings on January 6, 1960 when the last flight returned to Oakland, and the huge Boeing Stratocruiser taxied to the end of the field to join the fleet now at rest.

Yet nearly three decades later, former employees of the airline—janitors, guards, secretaries, executives, mechanics, and flight crew members—recall the years they spent with Transocean Air Lines as the best years of their lives.

To tell all of the exciting tales from those storybook days in this one volume is impossible. This work is not intended to be an exhaustive history of the airline but more a summary for the enjoyment of the casual reader and a stimulus for those who were a part of it to recall and relive their experiences.

My goal has been to provide in words and photographs at least a partial record of a great airline, its visionary and charismatic founder, Orvis Marcus Nelson, and the unique group of people who were, in fact, Transocean Air Lines.

I hope I have succeeded.

Arue Beaulieu Szura

Acknowledgements

When I determined to write the story of Transocean Air Lines five years ago, I was blissfully unaware of the complexity of the task ahead. Were it not for the generosity of nearly one hundred of my fellow ex-Transoceanites, plus many other aviation buffs (some of whom I have not met), and the assistance and enthusiasm of my editor, Kin Millen of Castro Valley, California, this book could not have been completed.

Several former Transocean employees supplied photographs from their collections. Most of the pictures used in this book are from the collection of Ralph Lewis of Grass Valley, California, radio operator and company photographer for Transocean Air Lines. Also shown are a number of photographs from the collection of H.G. "Red" Emery, now deceased, who was for several years the station manager at Transocean's Wake Island base. It is our good fortune that Red was a packrat, par excellence. During the final days of the airline, Red apparently grabbed whatever was at hand and hauled it to his San Ramon, California, home for safekeeping. For nearly a quarter of a century this cache of Transocean Air Lines' memorabilia and photographs reposed in the dilapidated chicken coop in Red's back yard until it was discovered by the author in time to be included in this book.

Other rare photographs that enriched this story came from the collection of William T. Larkins of Pleasant Hill, California. More than fifty years of Oakland International history has been captured on film by Mr. Larkins.

I am especially grateful to Edith Nelson, R.E.G. Davies, Sherwood A. Nichols, William R. Rivers, Edward C. Landwehr, William L. Keating, and Virginia MacKenzie for their careful reading of the manuscript for accuracy and their invaluable suggestions for enhancing the story. Ed Landwehr along with Bill Larkins and Newell Davis also spent much time researching aircraft for the section about Transocean's fleet.

Other friends and employees of Transocean, too numerous to mention in this space, have also contributed to bring this project to fruition. Thank you for your assistance in providing pieces to the story of Transocean.

Among those who were not employees but friends of Transocean who deserve special mention are Jon Proctor, David McQueen and John Wegg for their information about the Transocean fleet, Barbara Duncan, Beth Jacobs, Jerry Archer, Robin Worthington, Ray Orrock, Charles Mehrten, Helen Motroni, Maxine George, Marion Lego, and Lois Lack. Each one offered unlimited support and encouragement to the author.

My appreciation goes to my husband, Mike, who gave his unwavering support during the five years it took to complete the work; to my mother, Doris Beaulieu; and to my children and grandchildren. Last but not least my thanks to Stan Cohen for publishing such a beautiful book to honor the memory of Orvis Nelson and his great airline.

ORVIS MARCUS NELSON— MR. TRANSOCEAN

Not only was Orvis Nelson one of the most innovative and daring aviators and corporate giants active during the 1940s and 1950s, he was considered by many to be the most charismatic. Nelson also possessed the rare ability to command respect and undying loyalty from his employees. Because he never failed to convey by word and deed his confidence in the ability of each one to meet any challenge and get the job done, he inspired everyone to do their best.

Born in Tamarack, Minnesota, on March 18, 1907, Orvis was the second child born to Mamie and Marcus Nelson. He was preceded by his sister Myrtle. Nelson's father was a prosperous storekeeper who later went into a lumber business that eventually comprised several lumber tracts and sawmills. In the tradition of the hardworking Scandinavian families who settled in Minnesota, Nelson was exposed early on to the hard work and diligence of his parents. Out of this boyhood developed a man of character and determination. Those traits would later play a paramount role in his quest to succeed.

Charles Lindbergh and his parents were acquaintances of the Nelsons. It was "Lucky Lindy's" flight across the Atlantic in the spring of 1927 that captured Orvis' imagination. That association eventually led to his own entry into the world of aviation in the service of the Army Air Corps upon graduation from both Randolph and Kelly Fields by 1933.

Nelson was flying as a captain for United Air Lines when the United States entered World War II in 1941. He was assigned to fly for the Air Transport Command under a contract held by United. It was during a layover on the island of Okinawa, near the end of the war in 1945, that the idea for Orvis Nelson Air Transport (ONAT) was first conceived by Nelson and his fellow aviators.

On March 16, 1946, ONAT's first flight took off from Oakland Municipal Airport (now Oakland International Airport) to be in position on March 18 (Nelson's thirty-ninth birthday) to ferry a load of servicemen back to the U.S. from the Pacific war zones. This first flight was made just ten days before Nelson's marriage to Edith Frohboese, a United Air Lines stewardess.

On June 1, 1946, the date of the incorporation of the company, ONAT was renamed Transocean Air Lines. Transocean enjoyed fourteen years of incredible success but was forced into bankruptcy in early 1960 when beset by innumerable problems. Two of the most crippling were its inability to obtain the necessary financing and new aircraft to enter the jet age and the certification it desperately needed from the Civil Aeronautics Board to fly competing routes with the scheduled carriers.

The last Transocean Air Lines' airplane landed at the Oakland Municipal Airport on January 6, 1960. Nelson unsuccessfully continued his fight to obtain justice from the U.S. Government in the form of airline and route certification until his death in December 1976.

Orvis Marcus Nelson. DTC

REMEMBRANCES OF TRANSOCEAN AIR LINES
by Vivian Sims Kierson

I was hired as Orvis Nelson's secretary by Colonel Elsmore, who told me that Mr. Nelson was on his honeymoon. I reported for work at ONAT on April 4, 1946 as one of the first female employees of the company. Esther Lavagnini and Patricia Olesten were already working. So began a long and exciting experience.

Mr. Nelson, like all of the pilots-turned-executive that I've worked for, did not like desk work. Consequently, more often than not, correspondence had to be taken care of after regular office hours. Many times we worked until ten or eleven at night. Occasionally, we would go to the Nelsons' home in San Lorenzo to have dinner with Edith, but most often we just skipped eating. Food was not a priority in Orvis Nelson's life.

Over the years I made several trips with Mr. Nelson because he wanted me to take notes and type up proposals on the spot. One of these was to Tel Aviv for negotiations with the Israelis concerning Transocean's setting up an airline for them. I spent most of my time in Tel Aviv in an upstairs room off the restaurant of the hotel typing copious notes. On Saturday, the Jewish Sabbath, Mr. Nelson arranged for cars and a guide to take some of the crew members, TAL's Tel Aviv secretary, and me on a tour and then on to Jerusalem. We were not able to visit Bethlehem as it was surrounded by barbed wire and armed guards.

In Jerusalem, we stayed at the King David Hotel which had recently been bombed (by Begin's guerillas, I heard), and one side of the lobby had been blown out and was covered by a tarpaulin. When we returned to Tel Aviv on Sunday evening, I took a flight home, with a short layover in Geneva. The boss remained in Tel Aviv.

On the flight across the Atlantic I was pressed into service as a flight attendant and was embarrassed when we ran out of food before all of the passengers had been fed. There was a male flight attendant on board, but, being the female half, I was given the job of cooking the meal. Yes, we actually cooked on the aircraft, even if it did consist of opening cans, and heating the contents. That day's meal was to be beef stew, and we'd checked the supply and determined that we had plenty. But it turned out that one can that had no label, but was marked "stew," proved to be fruit cocktail. We finally located a can of carrots and some small cans of other vegetables and managed to eke out enough to serve everyone. What a joy it was for the flight attendants when our aircraft were finally equipped with warming ovens and already-prepared-meals were provided. But I can remember the days of box lunches, too. The airline catering business has come a long way.

I recall that one of the flights out of Oakland carried a load of refugees for the International Refugee Organization, among whom were some Chinese fleeing the Chinese Communists and were on their way to different destinations. Several wanted to go to Mexico, but when we landed in Brownsville, Texas, Mexican Immigration personnel found that only two of the Chinese had proper documentation for Mexico. Mr. Nelson took them on to Havana, hoping that the Cuban authorities might accept them along with the people who had Cuban passports. But they would not. The airplane then went to Panama where the remaining passengers were off-loaded to be flown by Panagra to their various Central and South American destinations. The Chinese without proper passports were taken back to California, and then returned to Hong Kong to take their chances dodging the communists.

I'd gone on this flight to take dictation while Mr. Nelson negotiated with the Cubans about forming an airline for them. While I was taking notes during the meeting with the Cubans in the hotel room, the flight crew members were out sightseeing. Then something happened to upset the Cubans. Perhaps we didn't have the proper landing documents. Anyway, Mr. Nelson told me

Colonel Ray T. Elsmore, Vivian Sims, May 1946. VSK

to round up the flight crew; that we were to leave Cuba immediately. He said that if we weren't airborne within an hour, the aircraft would be impounded and we would all be put in jail.

He next sent me to Pan American's catering kitchen to get food for the passengers while the flight crew completed flight plans, fueling, and preflight procedures. Because I knew only a few words of Spanish, communication with the kitchen help was poor. In addition, they seemed to think it was all a big joke and kept teasing me instead of doing what I was telling them to do. By the time I

-ix-got the box lunches, we had about five minutes to get off the ground. We left right on our deadline.

I've since wondered if the Cubans actually gave us that deadline, or if Mr. Nelson was pulling a fast one on us. Whatever it was, it worked. We'd had visions of spending time in Cuba's dungeons which the crew members had seen on their sightseeing tour. Anyway, Mr. Nelson remained in Cuba, I assumed to continue his negotiations, which eventually broke down. The Cuban airline was formed without our help.

THE WAY IT WAS
by Jeanne Lattanner

From a letter to friends, July 10, 1947. Jeanne was the director of personnel for Transocean Air Lines, 1946-1948.)

The day before one of Transocean's planes was to leave for Rome, Italy, on a charter flight, Mr. Nelson (who was to be the pilot) told me that if I had my passport and visas he would take me along as stewardess. That was enough for me! I took the afternoon off and went to San Francisco to get the documents. Twenty-four hours later, I had all the paperwork, my smallpox and typhus shots, and was on the airplane heading for Rome. Two of TAL's vice presidents were aboard — Sherwood Nichols, who was the radio operator, and Doug Johnson was flying as navigator.

On board were thirty-eight passengers (one was a month-old baby, another was a bullfighter) who were bound for Madrid and Rome to visit relatives they had not seen since before World War II ended. Feeding all those people was no easy chore, and afterward I had to wash all those dinner trays in a tiny sink!

From Oakland we flew to Chicago for refueling, then on to New York City where we had a three-day layover before leaving for Europe. I hardly saw my room at the Commodore Hotel on 42nd Street — I figured I could sleep when I returned home! Some of the crew and their wives and I were on the go all the time. We went to the Starlite Roof of the Waldorf Astoria Hotel, Ruban Blue, the Stock Exchange, Statue of Liberty, and then rode through Central Park in the middle of the night in a horse-drawn carriage. But we did manage to catch about three hours of sleep before departure time.

We were routed through Gander, Newfoundland, to Shannon, Ireland, where we arrived at 4:00 in the afternoon and circled the field, awaiting our turn to land. The countryside was lush and green, sparsely populated; each parcel of land fenced by low growing trees. Here and there stood the remains of a once great castle, usually situated on a small hill in the middle of a grove of trees.

After we landed, a uniformed Irish girl came aboard to welcome us to Ireland in Gaelic. Inside, the airport building was lovely; well furnished with red plush chairs, red carpeting and red velvet drapes, not all green as one would expect, and the crew was served dinner at a table set with fine china, crystal, and silver.

From Shannon we flew straight to Madrid, but the airway pattern first led us across Portugal, and Mr. Nelson flew low over Lisbon a couple of times at two thousand feet so we could get a look at the city. It's nice when the president of the airline is your pilot! We then continued on our way to Madrid, about a six hour flight from Shannon. We flew at between 8,000 and 9,000 feet altitude; above that we would have required oxygen.

Our bullfighter passenger became so excited when we flew over the main bullring in Madrid that he ran up and down the aisle of the plane shouting for joy to be home again. We landed at Barajas Airport in time for a breakfast of fruit, and steak with an egg on top! Never have that at home!

Eva Peron was to arrive from Argentina the next day to see the Pope, and the airport building had been adorned with the most elaborate decorations I had ever seen.

While in Madrid, we met our other deluxe Transocean DC-4 which had left San Francisco a few days before us and flown to Madrid via Manila, India, Egypt, and Italy.

Madrid is a hilly city, and the streets downtown are not wide; in fact, the sidewalks are so narrow that we had to walk single file. Almost all of the women wore black dresses, which I found very depressing. And lots of soldiers — none of whom wore shoes — were marching up and down. Nobody spoke English as there had been few tourists there since the war, and little opportunity to practice.

I hated to leave Madrid so soon, but by late afternoon we were back on the plane and on our way to Rome, where the airport buildings and airplane hangars at Rome were still in ruins. We drove into Rome on the Via Appia and checked in at the old Majestic Hotel on Via Veneto. The building had not been improved since years before the war, but the elevator, with its ornate iron grillwork, was a work of art. I was given the tiniest room, with no bath, but from the balcony I had a wonderful view of the city.

While we were walking down the streets on our way to dinner at the Cafe New York—wouldn't you know, not Italian at all—we were constantly trailed by small boys about seven or eight years old who begged for cigarettes which they would sell to make money.

The weather was balmy and warm; the night sky full of bright stars. After dinner, we rode in a carriage up the Via Veneto hill to a nightclub which at first appeared to be a low stucco wall. But inside it was a natural arena, with tables on each terrace, and completely canopied by trees. At the bottom was a marble dance floor where two orchestras played and wonderful Flamenco dancers performed.

On Sunday, we went to the Vatican and I thought of all the Movietone Newsreels I'd seen showing the Pope on his balcony in front of the masses of people filling Vatican Square. But that Sunday it was almost empty except for several little girls all dressed in white who had just made their First Communions. We drove on to the Piazza Venezia and the old Palace, where we saw the balcony from which Mussolini had made so many speeches. The city of Rome was very clean; there were no tossed papers anywhere, and we were told that Mussolini had seen to it that the streets were immaculate, and that he had also repaired some of the old ruins.

A visit to Rome would not have been complete without a visit to the Coliseum. Nearby there were street vendors selling cameos. Some of them spoke English and told us that they had previously lived in the United States for many years before retiring to Italy to live comfortably on their Social Security checks!

Although our stay was short, we did manage a quick drive past the beautiful old Castle St. Angelo before heading for the airport to fly a planeload of Italian seamen to New York City where they would become the crew of a ship sailing back to Italy. Their captain, whom we heard had had two ships blown out from under him during World War II, flashed a most unusual set of aluminum teeth every time he smiled! Each sailor carried a bottle of Chianti in a raffia bag and a sack of oranges.

Our route took us across Sardinia and Elba, then straight north to Paris, where Mr. Nelson flew the plane very low over the Seine, Sacre Coeur, and the Eiffel Tower, and we were all wishing something would happen so we could land. But we didn't have landing rights, so he was taking a chance flying at one thousand feet over the city. After a quick turn back and forth, we got away fast.

None of the passengers spoke English, but when they saw that I had to remove a cover in the tail of the plane to toss refuse down a large tube, then get down on my hands and knees on the floor to shove it through, they offered to do it for me during the rest of the flight. I was glad they were so friendly. Looking straight down at the ocean eight thousand feet below was scary!

During our two-day layover in New York City we went to the roof of the Astor Hotel, where Carmen Cavallaro was appearing, and then spent one afternoon "tea dancing" to the music of the Vincent Lopez Orchestra at the Taft Hotel before winging our way back to Oakland nine days after we had departed on what turned out to be a wonderful, never-to-be-forgotten trip. I wouldn't have missed it for the world!

Left to right: Jimmy Doak, Jeanne Lattanner and Samuel L. Wilson, Honolulu, 1947. RL

PHOTOGRAPH SOURCES

FA	Frances Atoigue collection	MIS	Mac Iver Studio
CB	Carl Barefield collection	FK	Frances Kenny collection
WB	W. Barnett collection	VSK	Vivian Sims Kierson collection
KB	Ken Bo's Studio	LP	Laing Photos
BA	Boland Associates	WTL	William T. Larkins
BS	Burris Studio	LPS	Leo's Photo Studio
C	Cinesound, Ltd.	RL	Ralph Lewis
BC	Bill Cogan	McC	Ether McConnell collection
DTC	Douglas T. Cole collection	RM	Royal Minson collection
CS	Columbia Studio	AEM	A.E. Morjig collection
HC	Harriet Corbett collection	RGM	Richard G. Mueller
CLC	C.L. Curtis collection	EN	Edith Nelson collection
ND	Newell Davis collection	WO	William Oliver collection
WD	William Dell collection	EP	Ed Peiffer collection
DD	Doris Dooley collection	PO	Port of Oakland
RD	Roger Dudley	PR	Pete Rayburn collection
NE	Nancy Edgerly collection	KRP	Ken Rice Photo
BE	Burt Elliott collection	RP	Rothschild Photo
HGE	H.G. Emery collection	JR	John Russell collection
EI	Enell, Inc.	SP	Stanart Photo
FC	Art Forde & Fred Carter	LSS	Lawrence S. Smalley
LNF	Lesley N. Forden collection	FS	Frank Soares collection
HF	H. Frank	AS	Arue Szura collection
CG	C. Gallop	TNM	Taloa News Magazine
DG	David Gregory collection	BT	Bud Thuener
CGC	Clint Groves collection	TWN	Transocean World News
AH	Albert "Kayo" Harris	TNS	Travel News Service
HOP	Herrington-Olson Photography	WPS	Walt's Photo Service
HAP	Honolulu Airport Photographers	YDR	Yakima Daily Republic

DEDICATION

For the People of Transocean Air Lines
and
Their Families
For
Michael Szura, Jr.
With a Special Tribute to Edith Nelson

To the Memory of Orvis Marcus Nelson
Founder and President of Transocean Air Lines

Also to the memory of Dorothy Mehrten,
Ol' Uncle Bert Crampton, Oliver Rosto, and those
Transocean Air Lines friends who have "flown west" before us

Contents

CHAPTER ONE: The Purple Mission No. 75   1

CHAPTER TWO: Around the World with Transocean   11

CHAPTER THREE: The Daring Young Flight Crews   29

CHAPTER FOUR: Magic Carpet to Mecca   47

CHAPTER FIVE: Wings Over Paradise   59

CHAPTER SIX: Land of the Northern Lights   81

CHAPTER SEVEN: TAL—The First Aviation Conglomerate   91

CHAPTER EIGHT: End of a Golden Age   121

AFTERWORD   139

APPENDIX   141

AIRPLANE LIST   146

BIBLIOGRAPHY   150

TAL DC-4 #N-90915, Oakland Int'l. Airport, May 1952. WTL

TAL Headquarters, Hangar 5, Oakland Municipal Airport, Oakland, California, 1948. RL

Chapter One: The Purple Mission No. 75
Prelude To a New Era

August 6, 1945

THE STREETS of Hiroshima, Japan, were crowded with workers and children hurrying to jobs or school in the warm morning sunshine. The sky over the city was bright blue and cloudless, yet few saw or heard the three airplanes flying in from the east. Those who did merely dismissed them as reconnaissance aircraft and continued on their way.

At precisely 8:15:17, a 9,000 pound atom bomb, dubbed "Little Boy," was released directly over the center of the city from the bomb bay of a United States B-29, *Enola Gay*. The air-raid sirens across the city began to wail almost simultaneously. There was a blinding flash of light, and in forty-three seconds, ten square miles of Hiroshima were obliterated. More than 130,000 people perished, of whom ten were American prisoners of war held in Hiroshima Castle. Most of those captives were crewmen who had bailed out of the *Lonesome Lady*, a B-24 bomber hit by flak on July 28 during a mission to sink Japan's last battleship, the *Haruna*, docked in Kure Harbor near Hiroshima.

The bomb's firestorm scorched everything within five miles of ground zero. The temperature at the center of the blast was estimated to be nearly 50 million degrees centigrade, or about three times greater than the temperature at the center of the sun. Those who survived screamed in agony from the excruciating pain of their burns as a huge mushroom-shaped cloud boiled upward over a grotesque landscape that spoke of death and destruction.

Word of the catastrophe did not reach Tokyo until noon that day because communication lines were wiped out. The sketchy news astonished and confused Emperor Hirohito and members of the Japanese cabinet. They were unable to believe that so much destruction could have been caused by a single bomb.

War Minister General Korechika Anami sent an inspection team, headed by Professor Yoshio Nishina and supported by other nuclear physicists, to Hiroshima. Nearly two and a half days later, they returned to Tokyo. Nishina appeared to be in shock as he described the "unspeakable scene" and confirmed what they had most feared: The United States now had an atomic weapon capable of annihilating every city in Japan within hours.

August 9, 1945.

A meeting of the Supreme War Council was held at 10:30 a.m. with the emperor presiding. Heated arguments dragged on interminably between die-hard militarists who believed Japan should fight to the end and those who favored peace through surrender.

At 11:01, midway through the meeting, a B-29 named *Bock's Car* dropped a second atom bomb, "Fat Man," on Nagasaki, leveling most of the city and killing 35,000 of its inhabitants. Still, the dissension continued late into the night among the members of the council.

Finally, Admiral Kantaro Suzuki, in an unprecedented break with the constitution, asked the emperor to express his wishes. Hirohito, whose traditional role had been to agree, not advise, appeared drawn and shaken as he addressed the council: "I cannot bear to see my innocent people suffer any longer. The time has come when we must bear the unbearable. I swallow my own tears and give my sanction to the proposal to accept the Allied proclamation."

The stalemate was finally broken after a frantic discussion of surrender, but the long delay proved tragic. It had taken the devastation of two great cities to bring to an end the bloodiest war in the history of Planet Earth.

August 15, 1945 VJ-Day—Victory Over Japan

When the unconditional surrender of Japan was broadcast around the world, jubilant Americans poured into the streets of cities and towns across the nation to celebrate the long-awaited victory. But even before the street sweepers had finished scooping up the tons of confetti, banners, and signs left behind by the celebrants, U. S. ships and transport planes were already crisscrossing the Pacific, carrying occupation troops to Japan and bringing home the wounded and the dead.

Island Hopping in the Pacific

Several islands and atolls in the South Pacific—Hawaii, Johnston, Kwajalein, Wake, Guam, and Okinawa—had been used by the U.S. military during the war as steppingstone bases to crack the Japanese defense.

Okinawa, the island nearest to the Land of the Rising Sun, had been designated as the staging area for The Purple Mission No. 75. This was the code name for the landing, set for November 1, 1945, of the first wave of occupation troops. Servicemen, supplies, and what seemed to be every C-54 transport in the world had been amassed on the island in preparation for the invasion of Japan before the atom bomb had assured the U.S. of total victory in August.

The Air Transport Command (ATC) of the U.S. Army Air Corps now began ferrying flight crews to Honolulu to reestablish communications to the states and to organize a flying schedule to transport the mail and supplies needed for the occupation. Many of these flight crews had been recruited by the ATC from the ranks of commercial airlines, private pilots, crop dusters, even barnstormers, for just such a mission as far back as June 1942.

Captain Orvis Marcus Nelson, later to become the founder of Transocean Air Lines, was a veteran pilot flying for United Air Lines when the United States entered World War II in 1941. He had then been assigned to fly for the ATC under a contract held by United and was one of the civilians flying the C-54 four-engine transports in conjunction with The Purple Mission.

Destined to Fly

Nelson, who had been born in Tamarack, Minnesota in 1907 was the son of Marcus and Mamie Nelson. His father had been born in Grimstad, a small town on the southeast coast of Norway, but was brought to the United States while still an infant, the family settling in Tamarack, Minnesota. Orvis' mother was from a family that landed at Jamestown, the first English colonial settlement in America, prior to the American Revolutionary War. Several generations later, the family moved west and settled in Franklin, Indiana, where Mamie was born. Later, as young woman, she visited her married sister who was living in Tamarack. There she met and soon married Marcus, a prosperous storekeeper.

Orvis Nelson's sturdy Norwegian-American stock and the rugged discipline of working alongside his father in the northern woods throughout his childhood would stand him in good stead for the rest of his life. Nelson spent his last winter in Minnesota—the early months of 1927—working near Gull Lake, which is near the town of Brainerd, clearing out a Nelson timber tract.

During the spring of 1927, a young man named Charles "Lucky Lindy" Lindbergh, whose family was acquainted with the Nelsons, made the first solo nonstop flight from New York to Paris flying his Ryan NYP monoplane, *The Spirit of St. Louis*. The lanky, soft-spoken Lindbergh landed in triumph on May 21 at le Bourget airfield near Paris after the 3,600 mile flight of more than thirty-three hours. It was then that twenty-year-old Nelson, along with the hundreds of other American boys inspired by Lindbergh's accomplishment, began to think about a future in aviation. That same year, Nelson enlisted in the U.S. Army Air Corps as a private.

Nelson graduated from Chanute Field in Illinois and served in the Philippines before buying out of his enlistment to return to college. There he paid his way by doing aerial photography in rented Wacos and old Travel Airs. He later returned to the Air Corps and by the fall of 1933 had graduated from training at both Kelly Field and Randolph Field.

But Nelson eventually became discontented with the military and resigned to sign on as a copilot with United Air Lines (UAL) on July 1, 1935. By 1943, he was flying from Seattle to Alaska for the ATC under a UAL contract. The next year when Northwest Airlines assumed the ATC contract for the Alaska shuttle, Nelson and the other United pilots assigned to that operation were transferred to the United-ATC routes from San Francisco to the islands of the South Pacific.

Nelson was in flight between Guam and Kwajalein when the first atom bomb was unleashed over Japan, and between Kwajalein and Johnston

Island when the news of the bomb was broadcast. By the time he arrived at Honolulu there were indications that Japan might surrender, and he was directed to return his aircraft to Okinawa.

Grounded on Okinawa in mid-August, Nelson and several other United crewmen sat around talking, killing time while waiting for back-to-back typhoons to wear themselves out. In the group were Sid Nelson, who had been been active in the Air Line Pilots' Association with Orvis and who would become a director of TAL; Harry Huking, a senior United pilot; and radio operator Sherwood Nichols, destined to be secretary-treasurer and one of the original directors of the airline.

In the light of a single candle, with torrential rain and wind battering the canvas Army tent they occupied near the Yontan Airstrip, the conversation quickly turned to the usual topic—what to do after the war ended. Most of the men had had a taste of flying to exotic places in all the corners of the world, and they did not want to let go of that thrill. If at all possible, they wanted to continue flying for commercial airlines.

Nelson reasoned that it would undoubtedly be a long time before the Japanese would be permitted to have their own domestic airline, and he suggested that someone from the group propose to United Air Lines to either extend its routes across the Pacific to the Orient or organize a domestic airline in Japan. If either idea proved unacceptable to United management, Nelson felt that the next step should be to try to set up a Japanese airline themselves.

The men agreed with the plan and decided there in the tent to form an association. Each member agreed to put up money if and when the time came to do so. The name they chose was ONAT for Orvis Nelson Air Transport Company, and they elected Nelson their representative to contact United.

United's "Pat" Patterson rejected the proposal to extend its service to Hawaii or to establish a domestic airline in Japan. However, he did help Nelson by providing him with a letter of introduction to General Douglas MacArthur, the Allied Supreme Commander in charge of the reconstruction of Japan and from whom permission for the venture would be required.

Nelson then went to an old friend, Colonel W.E. "Dusty" Rhoades, who had been MacArthur's personal pilot throughout the war, and asked him to explore the project with the general in Tokyo. The answer was again discouraging. MacArthur rejected the proposal, saying he thought it inadvisable to set up an American carrier in Japan until a formal peace treaty was signed. Disappointed by his failure to interest either United or MacArthur in their plans, Nelson shelved the Okinawa group's idea.

ONAT—First a Dream; Now an Airline

Newspaper headlines in 1946 were packed with tension: "U.S. Joins in Pacification of Manchuria," "Russ Seek World Domination," "Iranian Crisis Near Breaking Point."

That same year, Deanna Durbin and Dorothy Lamour were the reigning queens on movie screens, and at the grocery store housewives paid twenty-four cents a pound for steaks and pot roast; bread was eight cents a loaf, and coffee sold for thirty-one cents a pound. But vacationers who could afford to fly to Hawaii paid a hefty $648 for a round-trip ticket from San Francisco aboard a Pan American Clipper.

By early March, Nelson was back flying United's Denver-to-San Francisco route when he received a call from Jack Herlihy, vice-president in charge of operations for UAL. Herlihy asked Nelson how soon he could organize a flying operation in the Pacific for the ATC under a subcontract from United to provide twice-daily transport service between Hamilton Field near San Francisco, and Hickam Field, Hawaii. Nelson jumped at the opportunity without concern for "how soon." He knew he could do it.

Herlihy offered to lend key personnel to begin the organization and told Nelson that negotiations were already under way for the lease of twelve surplus U.S. Air Force C-54s. Then he issued a nearly impossible demand: position the first airplane in Honolulu in time for a return flight to the West Coast on March 18. This meant that Nelson, a pilot without an airplane or a hangar to put it in, had just ten days to construct an airline.

Nelson began moving at top speed within seconds after his conversation with Herlihy. He first called his wartime radio operator, Sherwood Nichols, who was then working as a station attendant for United at Boise, Idaho. Nichols immediately agreed to join Nelson as chief of communications.

The next items on Nelson's agenda were to locate the rest of the Okinawa group, borrow the United men Herlihy had promised, place classified ads for flight crews in the San Francisco and Los Angeles newspapers, and then telephone Hamilton

Field to inform them he was in business. To his surprise, this news had already reached the installation earlier in the day. Base personnel told Nelson that some fifty demobilized pilots were already on their way to apply for jobs.

Several thousand telephone calls for Nelson were received at his San Lorenzo, California, home during the first twenty-four hours of his search for flight crews, setting a record at the local telephone company for the most calls ever routed to a residence.

On March 11, 1946, Nelson terminated his employment with United Air Lines and then attended a conference sponsored by the ATC staff for United Air Lines and the other subcontractors on the transpacific project.

General Bob Nowland presided over the discussion. Nowland, who was then the commanding general of the Pacific Wing of the ATC, had been a first lieutenant in Nelson's Army Air Corps outfit in the Philippines in 1928 and 1929. Colonel Ray T. Elsmore, another prominent officer at the conference, had once been employed by Western Air Lines, had practiced law, and had been a pilot for the U.S. Postal Service.

Elsmore had served as Director of Air Transport, Allied Air Forces in the Southwest Pacific, under General George C. Kenney during World War II. On active duty since 1940, Elsmore had been in the Philippines when the Japanese invaded the islands but had managed to escape to Australia on the last airplane out. He subsequently directed troop-carrier ATC operations in the Pacific.

When General Douglas MacArthur began his military campaign up the New Guinea Coast, the only air route for flying supplies to him was over the Owen Stanley Range in the southeastern end of the island. When a shorter route became imperative to keep Air Transport abreast of MacArthur's advances, Elsmore flew a tour of inspection to chart an alternate route.

One of these flights took him over the Grand Valley, known also as Hidden Valley or Shangri-la. In May of 1945, a military transport airplane crashed on the high palisades over the Hidden Valley. The airplane had been carrying twenty-four military personnel, three of whom were members of the Women's Army Corps (WAC). Five of the passengers survived the crash, including the three WACs. Within twenty-four hours, two of the WACs died of injuries sustained in the accident, but the other WAC and two servicemen miraculously lived.

Ray T. Elsmore, executive vice-president, Transocean Air Lines. HGE

Elsmore directed a daring rescue using gliders to fly out the survivors from that isolated valley. A transport airplane dropped medical corpsmen and engineers by parachute to the valley floor to bring relief to the injured and to construct a landing strip on which a glider could be safely landed and be picked up again by a low-flying transport plane. Other airplanes dropped food, medical supplies, and other necessities by parachute. Nearly seven weeks passed from the time of the crash until operations had progressed enough to permit a glider pickup of the trio and their rescuers.

Nelson was impressed with Elsmore's demeanor and military and commercial flying record and hired him on the spot as his chief assistant. Elsmore soon would carry the title of executive vice-president of ONAT.

When Nelson returned to his San Lorenzo home that night, he was greeted by a large group of pilots, copilots, radio operators, navigators, flight engineers, and operations men filling his front porch and milling around in front of his house. Most were hired that night, including William

Orvis M. Nelson, president of Transocean Air Lines; Ray T. Elsmore, executive vice-president of Transocean Air Lines, 1946. VSK

Word, who would become a flight captain for ONAT, and Harvey Rogers, later to be chief pilot of the airline.

United loaned Navigator Roland Halper, Navigator Al Mays, Mechanic Al Carvel, and Flight Engineer Jim McCoy. Ted Vinson, former Consairways pilot, became the airline's first chief pilot.

The hiring of Sam Wilson, Wally Simpton, and Art Bisset was typical of the flamboyant way Nelson gathered his personnel. Wilson was still in the Air Corps but had decided to make the switch to civilian life when he heard of Nelson's "start-up" airline in March, 1946. He called the local United Air Lines office for information and waited while someone there telephoned Nelson's home. When Nelson answered, Wilson got on the line:

"I hear you're looking for pilots," said Wilson.

"Yes," replied Nelson. "You looking for a job?"

"Maybe," said Wilson cautiously.

"O.K.—you're hired."

This seemed a little abrupt to Wilson. "Don't you even want to see my logbook?" he asked.

"Hell, no—I've heard all about you."

"Well . . . say, Nelson, there's another fellow here who's looking for a pilot's job—name of Wally Simpton."

"Is he O.K.?" asked Nelson.

"Yes. . . ."

"O.K.—he's hired."

Bisset had just been discharged from the military when he spotted the "Flight Engineers Wanted" advertisement in a local newspaper and went to Oakland Municipal Airport (now Oakland International Airport) to check it out.

When Nelson asked what kinds of airplanes he'd flown, Bisset started to reply with B-17s and B-24s when Nelson interrupted to tell him he was hired.

The frenetic pace picked up. On Wednesday, March 13, Nelson and Captain W.W. "Pop" Warner headed for the San Francisco International Airport to receive the first of the twelve Army-owned C-54s to be leased to ONAT and ferry it across San Francisco Bay to Oakland.

No sooner had they taxied the aircraft to a stop when Nelson hurried off to find office space for the operation. He discovered that the old two-story stucco hotel at Oakland Municipal Airport (said to be the first airport hotel in the nation) was vacant and signed a lease with the Port of Oakland.

Oakland Municipal Airport had been the departure point for many of the early air races such as the Dole Pineapple Race on August 16, 1927. That year eight fliers competed for $35,000 in prize money offered by Jim Dole, so-called "Pineapple King" of Hawaii.

The Oakland Airport was also aviatrix Amelia Earhart's departure point on May 20, 1937 when she and her navigator, Paul Noonan, began their second attempt to circle the globe. The Lockheed lifted off from Runway 27 heading east. They hop-scotched across the country, landing at Tucson, New Orleans, and Miami. On June 1 they left Miami, stopping en route at such places as Caripito, Venezuela; Natal, Brazil; Fort Lamy, Chad, French Equatorial Africa; Calcutta, India; and Singapore. They were more than half way around the world when they landed at Lae, New Guinea, on June 30. On July second, after departing Lae, Amelia Earhart's plane vanished over the Pacific without even an oil slick.

A new era at the historic Oakland Airport was about to begin as Orvis Nelson Air Transport went into business. Soon veterans from all branches of the armed forces were queued in a long line stretching from the entrance, down the steps and to the tiny airport restaurant up the street. They looked as though they had just been discharged. Most were still dressed in their military uniforms and carrying duffel bags.

Nelson's "executive office" was bare except for a single telephone positioned in the middle of the floor. Between phone calls Nelson asked few questions of the men who came through his door to be interviewed and hired nearly every one of them.

Within several days Nelson had established the dispatch office, the chief pilot's office, and a room for communications and navigation personnel on the first floor. On the second floor he installed the payroll and accounting departments, a pilot's lounge for the standby crew, plus offices for the secretaries, Elsmore, and himself. The place hummed with activity and excitement.

Even Nelson's former bosses at United were caught up in the enthusiasm generated by the exuberant ONAT group. Jack Herlihy not only kept his word to Nelson for the loan of certain personnel but also persuaded UAL management to supply some of the needed office equipment and furniture, applications and other business forms. But most important, he provided two office managers to assist in creating office procedures and company policies.

On the eleventh day, after the ten days of "creation," Nelson rested. In that time, Nelson had managed to create the foundation for an airline that would eventually become the world's largest supplemental air carrier.

On the morning of March 16, 1946, the first flight departed for Honolulu in one of the leased C-54s. The ATC wanted the airplane to be in position in Honolulu to ferry to the U.S. mainland a load of military personnel returning from the South Pacific theaters of war on March 18, which was Nelson's thirty-ninth birthday. This was the inaugural flight of the ATC contract calling for two round trips daily between Hamilton Field, California, and Hickam Field, Hawaii. At the controls was Captain Jerry Byrd, a former Navy pilot. In the right seat was Jack Brissey, who had been one of the Air Corps' famous "Wilmington Warriors," the ferrying group for domestic and transatlantic flights during the war. Art Bisset, former Air Corps flight engineer, who had trained pilots in B-17s and B-24s during World War II, was the flight engineer. Bisset's meticulous attention to detail would later earn him the position of chief inspector for the airline. Ralph Lewis, violinist in the Lawrence Welk Orchestra before the war and a former radio broadcaster, was the radio operator. Al Mays, ONAT's first chief navigator, a soft-spoken southerner with a penchant for being precise in his calculations, was tabbed for that first flight.

Ten days after the historic first flight of ONAT, Nelson flew to New Jersey to marry Edith Frohboese, a petite blonde United Air Lines stewardess. Less than two hours after the wedding ceremony, the newlyweds were headed for California on a cross-country honeymoon by train.

Esther Lavagnini, an attractive, dark haired, twenty-two year old girl, was the first secretary of the airline. Esther came for her job interview dressed in an eye-catching black and white checked suit, high heels, and a wide brimmed black hat. She was greeted by a chorus of whistles and appreciative comments by the young aviators waiting outside the door.

Before many days had passed, Patricia Olesten and Vivian Sims were hired. Patricia's job was to type statistical reports; Vivian was to be Nelson's private secretary for many years.

Orvis Nelson with three crew members of TAL's first flight in March 1946. Left to right: Art Bissett, Ralph Lewis, Orvis Nelson and Jack Brissey. Captain Jerry Byrd not shown in photo. RL

-6-

TAL originals, 1946, left to right, front row: John Markusen, Jack Ullner, Louis Lombard, Sherwood A. Nichols, Ray T. Elsmore, William Word. Back row: Andrew McKelvie, Robert Walton, James Clarkson, Louis Sylvia, William R. Rivers, Ted Vinson, Orvis M. Nelson and Ray H. Elsmore. VSK

Others of the original ONAT office personnel and ground crew were William R. Rivers, Douglass F. Johnson, John Markusen, Jack Ullner, Louis Lombard, Don Sheets, Andrew McKelvie, and James Clarksen. This small band of employees, along with the flight crew members hired during that first month, forged the family-like bond that became the hallmark of the company through the years. Orvis Nelson had always admired the older pilots and held a certain fondness and admiration for them. Later, he would add such men as E.L. Sloniger, Colonel Benton "Lucky" Baldwin, and Chuck Sisto to the airline's roster.

ONAT was profitable from the start. In just two months the company netted nearly $70,000. But because income tax rates for individuals were high and as Nelson had no extraordinary expenses to write off, he decided to incorporate. A contest was held to name the new corporation. Ray Foster, a dispatcher at the headquarters, submitted the winning name. ONAT became Transocean Air Lines on June 1, 1946.

Nelson immediately sold $200,000 worth of stock and gave one percent to each department head and to the loyal members of the Okinawa group. His only personal outlay of cash was $1,000 down payment for a $25,000 insurance policy for his employees.

During the first months of operation, maintenance work was subcontracted to the Air Transport Division of the Matson Navigation Company at Oakland Airport. But with the quick growth of

TAL originals, 1946, left, bottom to top: Cecil "Pop" Bunbury, Ted Vinson, Joseph Stachon. Right: unidentified. HGE

Edith Nelson, first stewardess to fly across the Pacific after World War II, 1946. EN

Transocean, the corporation was able to secure quarters in a large hangar vacated by MATS and took over its own maintenance by the end of July.

Nelson had a clear concept of what was required of an airline to succeed in the post-war years: a carrier capable of supplementing and assisting the scheduled airlines; one with a high load factor, maximum utility and no frills; plus a system to secure return loads when needed in order to keep rates generally lower than other carriers. With this vision, Nelson and his team decided to enter the commercial contract field with company owned aircraft.

At the end of World War II, military surplus airplanes were available for purchase by veterans from the War Assets Administration of the U.S. government at a fraction of their real worth. Veterans Ray T. Elsmore and William L. Word, representing Transocean Air Lines, were among the first to receive their C-54s. Ownership of the four-engined transports would later be registered with the CAA in Transocean's name.

Ted Vinson, Bill Word, and Jim McCoy flew aircraft N66635 and N66644 from Walnut Ridge, Arkansas and Albuquerque, New Mexico, to a modification center in Southern California for CAA conversion from military to commercial configuration and for certification. By the time these two airplanes were purchased, Transocean was flying twelve government-leased planes on the San Francisco-Honolulu run.

With the arrival of the first two C-54s at Transocean's headquarters in Oakland, California, TAL began its rapid ascent into sunny skies. Several years would pass before Nelson would reflect on the irony that Transocean, conceived during a raging storm, would pass through innumerable squalls in its corporate life and end by being engulfed in a predatory tidal wave.

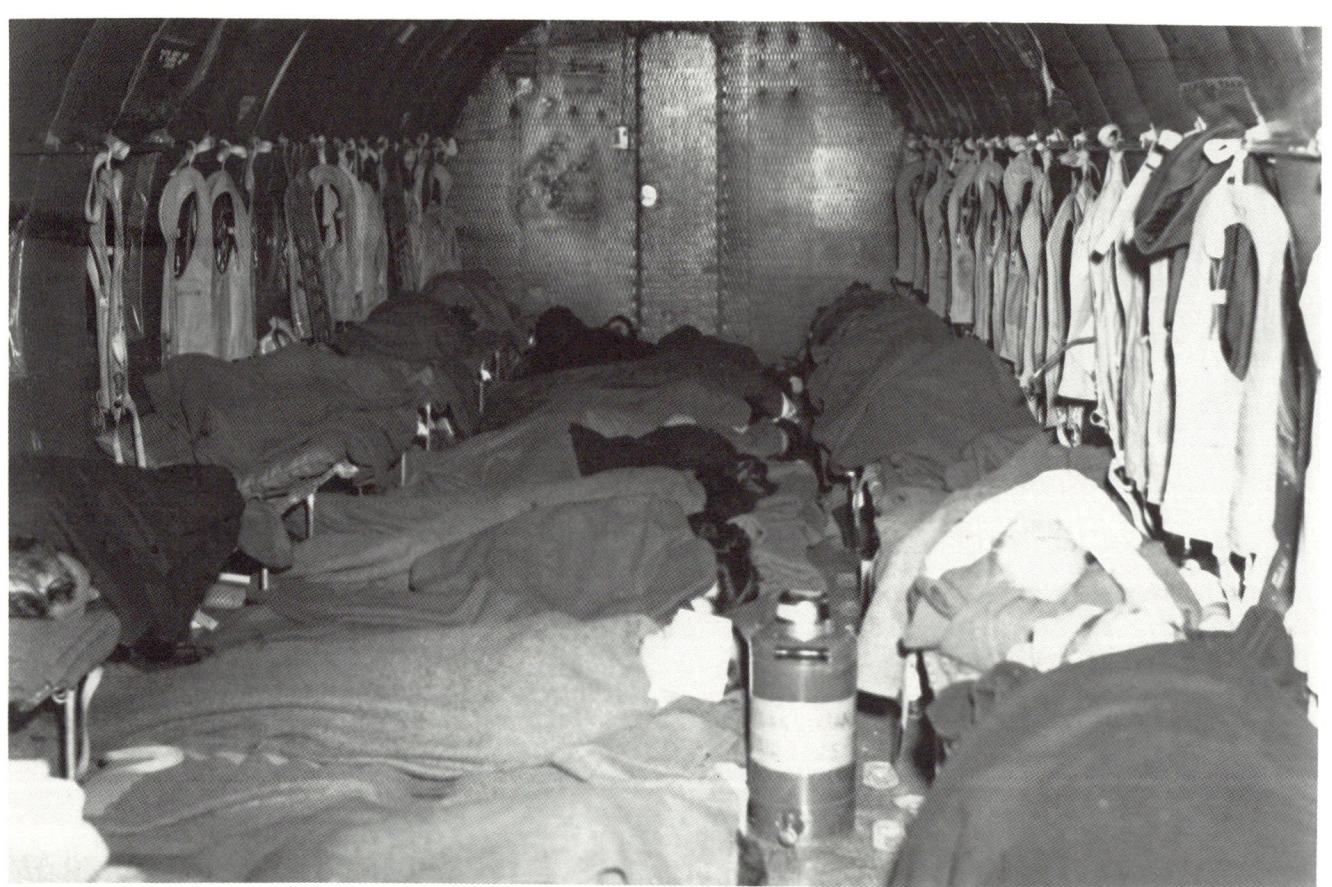

TAL's second flight, military personnel, 1946. RL

Left to right: Ted Vinson, Hank Severin, unidentified, Joe Stachon, Dan McCarthy, Cecil Bunbury, 1946. PO

Left to right: S.A. Nichols, Douglass Johnson, William Leonard, Orvis Nelson, S.L. Wilson, William Keating. Seated, Martha Jane Ekstrand. RL

TAL Headquarters, Hangar 5, Oakland Municipal Airport, Oakland, California, 1948. MIS

Chapter Two: Around the World with Transocean
Foreign Affairs

The Manila Connection

*F*ROM ITS earliest days Transocean Air Lines provoked concern and controversy among its competitors because of its unorthodox ways of getting business and its agility in completing its missions. Orvis Nelson and his crews were always ready and willing to leave for anywhere in the world on short notice with plane and payload.

"Every time I'd hear of a piece of business and go after it, there would be Nelson just departing, shaking hands in the doorway, the contract in his pocket," lamented one competitor. Another complained that every time Nelson threw the dice they came up seven; never snake-eyes.

"Sky tramps," "carpetbaggers of the skies," and "gypsies" were but a few of the labels or slurs put on the flight crews and their leader. The successful always have their detractors, and there were some among the scheduled carriers who considered Transocean an outcast in the world of aviation. But the name-calling merely added to the mystique already surrounding TAL and only helped to nurture the esprit de corps that was the most important asset of this adventurous airline.

Everyone expected Transocean to fail from the beginning and throughout its years of success. But history would show that it would be the bold young founders of this "crazy" airline who would make a significant contribution to modern air transportation.

The spirit of cooperation that existed within the organization would extend to governments and other airlines needing assistance during the hectic postwar years. Few countries in the Orient, Europe, or the Middle East had national airlines or airport facilities during the mid-forties. So Transocean often contracted with foreign governments to establish airlines, to supply management, and to train flight crews.

Transocean's first commercial contract was a round-trip charter between the U.S. mainland and the Philippines in June 1946, not long after the start of the ATC contract. Nelson negotiated with a Filipino newspaper publisher, a Dr. Yap, to fly to Manila a group of his countrymen who wanted to participate in the first Independence Day activities on the Fourth of July, 1946. But the modification center in Van Nuys, California, was unable to finish on schedule the conversion from cargo to passenger configuration of either of Transocean's two aircraft. As a consequence, TAL lost the job. The Philippine contingent had to find its own transportation to Manila. With help from Washington, D.C., most were able to hitch rides on ATC planes.

Finally, the conversion work on one of the C-54s was completed during the first week in July. Nelson sent it to Manila to bring the Yap Group back to the states. It turned out that Colonel Andres Soriano, president of Philippine Air Lines and owner of the San Miguel Brewery, had seen the TAL DC-4 leave Manila with Dr. Yap's passengers, and he called Nelson from Manila to find out if he would set up a transpacific charter service with him under Philippine Air Lines sponsorship. After Nelson paused briefly to contemplate the proposal, he and Soriano agreed on two trips. An extension of the contract would have to be preceded by further discussion.

Colonel Soriano wanted to start the charter service immediately. This news touched off a flurry of activity at Transocean's headquarters in Oakland. The airline's second C-54 was still undergoing modification to DC-4 standards in Southern California. The first aircraft, now back from Manila, was still equipped with bucket seats, and there was insufficient time to install regular

TAL-PAL crew car passing local transportation on the road between Manila and Santa Rosa, the Philippines. HGE

Philippine Air Lines DC-6 PI-C296 at Wake Island. HGE

During 1946, Transocean flew the first Commercial flight to Manila after World War II. TAL DC-4 N66635 flew the Pacific carrying the flags of both countries under a contract between TAL and Philippine Air Lines. WTL

Philippine Air Lines Crew House, Manila. TAL flight crew members, William Wakefield, unidentified, Herman Humm, 1947. RL

TAL flight crew members flying for Philippine Air Lines. Identities known: Joe Conn, John Kessing, Burr Hall, S.L. Wilson, De Witt Vernelson, John Hoenninger, Don Gallego, and Ralph Lewis. RL

passenger seats. On the night of July 22, the TAL employees were in high spirits as they set out to fix up the plane for the first trip under contract to Philippine Air Lines. Bill Rivers, the airline's new purchasing agent, spent the night on his knees padding the seats with foam rubber while Flight Engineer Jim McCoy fastened the headlining. People from administration, operations, maintenance, and several flight crew members assisted as needed. When their work was nearly completed, they put air mattresses aboard so the passengers could spread them out on the cabin floor and stretch out to sleep. Because Colonel Soriano would be meeting the flight, Nelson decided to fly the DC-4 himself. It would be a good time to cultivate their relationship and develop more business with Philippine Air Lines. His wife, Edie, accompanied him on the trip and served as stewardess.

It was morning before the last of the work had been finished on the DC-4, and it was ready to fly. Nearly every employee—even their husbands, wives, and children—showed up to give an enthusiastic send-off to the DC-4, which had been named *Miss Independence* for the Yap charter flight, now renamed *Taloa-Manila Bay* to honor the new service. The load consisted of thirty-five passengers and a small quantity of freight.

Transocean's first commercial flight gave the Philippines its first post-war air link with the United States. Edith Nelson had the distinction of being the first stewardess to complete the Pacific crossing for a commercial airline as Pan American employed only male stewards at the time.

Later, after Transocean sold PAL two DC-4s in return for a considerable block of stock in the Philippine airline, PAL canceled a contract it had given Trans World Airlines for the management of PAL's domestic runs on the islands and gave the contract to Transocean. United Air Lines lent to Transocean John Hodgson, one of their captains, who had been manager of United's Alaskan operation during the war, to go to the Philippines and establish the domestic division of PAL. He was in Manila for a year when Nelson sent Sam Wilson to take over the operation. Eventually, Nelson, Sherwood Nichols, and Ed Ringo worked out a contract with Soriano for the establishment and operation of a Philippine Air Lines international service to the United States, the Orient, and Europe.

In the months following those first flights to the Philippines, however, N66635, referred to within the airline as 635, was the most widely known and flown aircraft in the Pacific. During the late summer and fall of 1946, Aircraft 635 was the only commercial channel of communications between the United States and the Orient. This was because Pan American had suspended its operations and a maritime strike put the ships at anchor. That single DC-4 played a dual role carrying the flags of both the United States and the Philippines.

Adding to the mystique already surrounding Transocean were the quick-change paint jobs given 635 every time it arrived in Manila. As soon as the engines were shut down, a crew of painters would rush to paint over the TAL lettering to read "Philippine Air Lines" before departure time to the Orient. This created the impression along the route that Transocean had an entire fleet of aircraft servicing the South Pacific.

TAL Chief Pilot Harvey Rogers, Elpidio Quirino, vice president of the Philippines. RM

The TAL-PAL combination began service to Shanghai in September of 1946, and to Bangkok in November. On this route between Honolulu and Manila, Nelson used double crews, each crew consisting of captain, copilot, radio operator, navigator, and flight engineer. The first crew would fly the aircraft from Honolulu to Wake Island, where the second would take over en route to Guam. Then the first flight crew would again take command for the journey to Manila. After a twenty-four- to forty-eight-hour layover at each station, the two crews would alternate in flying the aircraft. Some flights would continue on from Manila to Shanghai, Bangkok, or Karachi. The double crew concept was a novel idea later to be used by other airlines.

"Taloa Manila Bay," at Guam. S.A. Nichols in doorway. Baggage handling is done a little differently today. RL

TAL's first DC-4, N66635. Changing names in Manila, 1946. 635 carried Philippine Air Lines' name from Honolulu, Wake, Guam, Manila and sometimes on to Shanghai. Before leaving Manila for the return trip to Honolulu, the name would be changed to Transocean Air Lines. RL

International Cooperation

During the early days of TAL, Nelson and Elsmore often served as pilots. On one of these flights, Nelson piloted a group of officials from the Philippine government and Philippine Airlines on a survey flight to Batavia, still at that time Dutch East Indies, (now Jakarta, Indonesia).

When Nelson landed, gunfire was erupting all around the airfield. The city was under seige by rebels. This forced Nelson to stop the refueling and get the DC-4 back in the air as quickly as possible. With full gas tanks in one wing and empty tanks in the other, the aircraft was pulling dangerously to one side. He kept the nose down and the control wheel locked in the opposite direction of the plane's yaw. Only with skill and a little luck was Nelson able to build up speed to get off the ground.

The second aircraft, N66644, was placed in schedule in October, 1946. A third, N79048, was put into service in January, 1947. The fourth, N95495, was acquired in November, 1946, was used for only one flight during the month of December prior to its conversion to a B model which was completed in April, 1947. These aircraft helped TAL during its first year in business to earn nearly one half million dollars with a capital investment of only $200,000.

Crew members served as Orvis Nelson's eyes and ears. Their support on several occasions inadvertently played into Lady Luck's hand for TAL. On one flight, a TAL plane with Philippine Air Lines painted on the fuselage developed leaks in the fuel tanks while on the Kwajalein-to-Guam leg. Because they were flying without cargo or passengers, Captain T. A. Buckelew elected to over-fly Guam and continue to the final destination, Manila.

Soon after passing their scheduled intermediate stop, Radio Operator Wally Barnett received a call from a frantic TAL station manager at Guam pleading for them to return to Guam. Apparently he had talked a salesman from rival Pacific Overseas Airlines into hitching a free ride with TAL instead of taking an earlier Pan American flight. This unintentional delay held the salesman in Guam while contract bids for flying services were being submitted and opened in Manila. Needless to say, TAL won that one.

Pakistan

In November 1947, Nelson headed for India and Pakistan looking for business. While in Calcutta he met with executives of Orient Airways to sell them three twin-engine C-47s and two twin-engine Beechcraft. Through these contacts Nelson and TAL became involved in the founding of Pak-Air, Ltd. This new airline was to serve Pakistan which had recently become self-governing, yet still within the British Commonwealth.

After many months of negotiations between Pak-Air and Transocean's Bill Rivers, a contract was forged to establish air service for Pakistan with the Haroon family, one of the ten wealthiest families in the world at the time. The agreement called for Transocean to provide Pak-Air with flight crews, operations and maintenance staffs for Pak-Air routes from Karachi to London and Singapore, and to assist in the establishment of domestic routes. TAL's Sam Wilson was sent to Karachi to assist the young airline in its operations. Later, when the Haroons decided they needed experienced management, Transocean was given the contract to run the airline.

But a crisis was already brewing when Flight Captain Dan McCarthy arrived in Pakistan in the spring of 1949 to relieve Sam Wilson from his TAL duties. Sam had been Transocean's first-in-command of their operations in Pakistan. The crisis began when many of the Pak-Air copilots felt they had served their apprenticeship and wanted to be checked out as captains. Some of these copilots had trained at the Taloa Academy of Aeronautics (a subsidiary of TAL at Oakland International), and some had flown in the Royal Indian Air Force. Still others had gained their experience flying domestic routes throughout India and Pakistan.

Captain McCarthy was distressed to find that most of the men who had not been previously trained at Transocean's academy were unqualified as copilots and immediately fired five of them as he feared they might cause an accident. The firing brought a swift and angry reaction from Pakistani pilots who promptly complained about their termination to relatives who were among the principal investors.

The administration of the airline had been delegated by the Haroon family to Hussain Malik, a Pakistani lawyer and a graduate of Cambridge University in London. Malik conceded that McCarthy was right in principle, but he was under substantial pressure from the Pakistani investors. Finally, he directed McCarthy to put the pilots back on flying status with the airline.

Captain McCarthy immediately canceled Transocean's management contract. An orderly transfer of management was accomplished over the next thirty days. This was with the understanding that TAL would no longer assume responsibility for the operation.

Ten days following TAL's pullout, a Pak-Air DC-3 with a full load of passengers crashed on a mountaintop during a flight from Calcutta to Karachi, killing all on board. At the controls were two of the pilots McCarthy had fired. They had apparently miscalculated the force of the wind and descended too soon on an estimated time of arrival (ETA) over Karachi.

Air Djibouti-Air Jordan, the Formative Years

The year was 1949. The governor of French Somaliland was envious of Ethiopian Air Lines and the British Aden Airways flying in and out of Djibouti with big cargo loads. But French Somaliland had no money, and France gave little encouragement for the country's future. The governor asked John Russell, a Trans World Airlines (TWA) employee then serving as operations manager for Ethiopian Air Lines, if he would form a national airline using the name Air Djibouti.

"We would be the carrier for the country, and this would provide us the necessary reciprocal landing rights in foreign countries," said Russell. "The possibilities of using C-46s for cargo were apparent to lower the ton/mile cost.

"Ethiopian Air Lines wasn't interested in using C-46s because they practically had a monopoly with their DC-3s and could charge any price to transport the number one cargo of khat, a fresh green leaf which the Arabs chewed, producing a narcotic effect.

Left to right: unidentified, TAL Captain W.W. Douglas, unidentified, Hussain Malik, Pak-Air, Ltd., unidentified, TAL Captain Cecil Hallinan, and TAL Navigator Don Fraim. RGM

Standing, left to right: Douglass Johnson, Ray T. Elsmore, William R. Rivers. Seated: Hussain Malik, Orvis M. Nelson and Mrs. Malik. RGM

Pak-Air, Ltd. aircraft, Pakistani visitors, TAL flight crew. AH

"Bill Pearce, who was with Ethiopian in Addis Ababa, and I decided to look for financing for Air Djibouti. We found a listener in Orvis Nelson of Transocean Air Lines.

"One of the reasons Nelson was willing to proceed was that our government was offering new C-46s, including spares, for $300 a month with the latest Pratt & Whitney engines and three bladed props, not the troublesome Curtiss Electra props previously used.

"We started with two aircraft (one had 3.4 hours flying time, the other 4.5 hours) and modified them at Transocean's base at Bradley Field, Connecticut.

"Bill Glenn and I took the second plane over in midwinter. We had an engine change at Goose Bay, Labrador, with two feet of snow on the ground. Glenn, with the help of the military, did the job in less than two days in sub-freezing temperatures, which was an outstanding feat.

"Our next stop was at Thule Air Force Base in Greenland, then continued to Shannon, Ireland, and on to Rome, where we picked up my wife and ten-month-old daughter and flew to Asmara, Eritrea, on the Persian Gulf. This was to be our home base as it was under the control of the United Nations and because there was no housing available at Djibouti.

"Verne Shrewsbury, who had preceded us with the first C-46, had everything organized on our arrival."

From its headquarters in Asmara, Air Djibouti DC-3s ferried fresh meat and vegetables from the plentiful East African plateau country to the desert outposts of Saudi Arabia, its capital city, Riyadh, and to the Arabian-American Oil Company (ARAMCO) installations around Dhahran.

Air Djibouti airplanes also transported cargo and conducted (in conjunction with Nairobi Air Services of Nairobi, East Africa) big game camera or shooting safaris from Saudi Arabia to the Nairobi area. Brochures advertising the tour service stated that Air Djibouti could fly passengers to "the exciting land of safaris, trout fishing, sailing, surf bathing, underwater fishing, and glamorous evenings in just twelve hours—ten times faster than the old Magic Carpet record."

The operation also flew religious pilgrims from Kabul, Afghanistan, to Jeddah, Saudi Arabia. From Jeddah they would continue to Mecca on foot because non-Moslems were not allowed in the holy city. The crews had to carry five-gallon or thirty-gallon drums of gasoline to have fuel for the return leg to Asmara after delivering the hajjis home, which was quite a logistic problem.

"In the middle of this operation I received a cable stating that the government of French Somaliland had been overthrown and that the governor had been assasinated. It closed with the command: DO NOT LAND IN DJIBOUTI.

"Three countries—Egypt, Lebanon, and Jordan—were considered as possible bases from which to operate our charter business since we were no longer able to land in Djibouti.

"A certificate was available in the name of Lebanese International Airlines in Lebanon, and in Jordan an established airline, Air Jordan (owned by His Excellency Ismail Bilbeisi Pasha), was

Air Djibouti C-46. JR

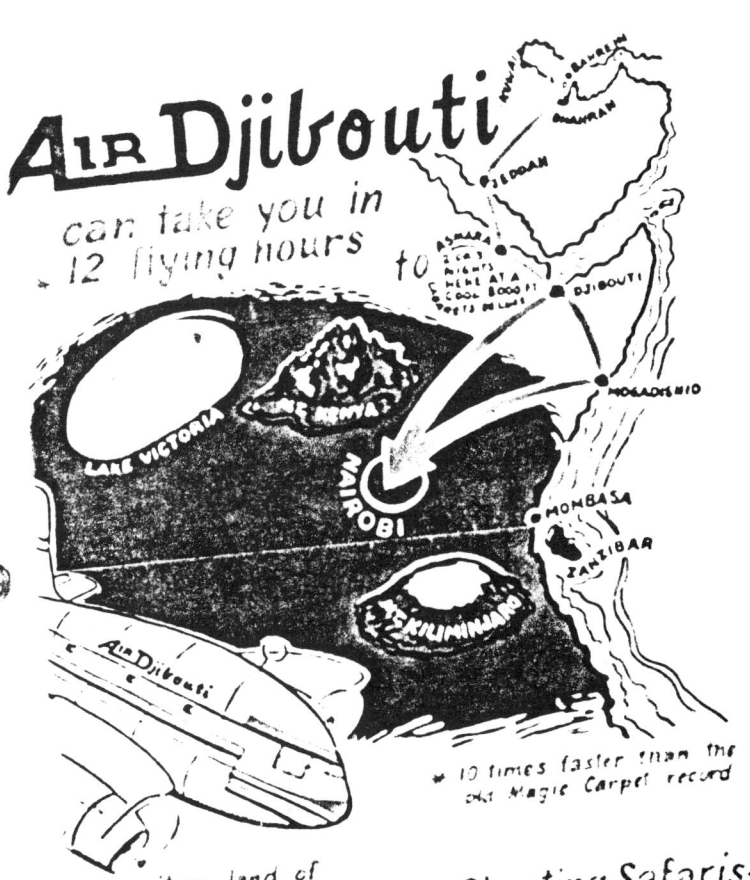

Air Djibouti advertisement. JR

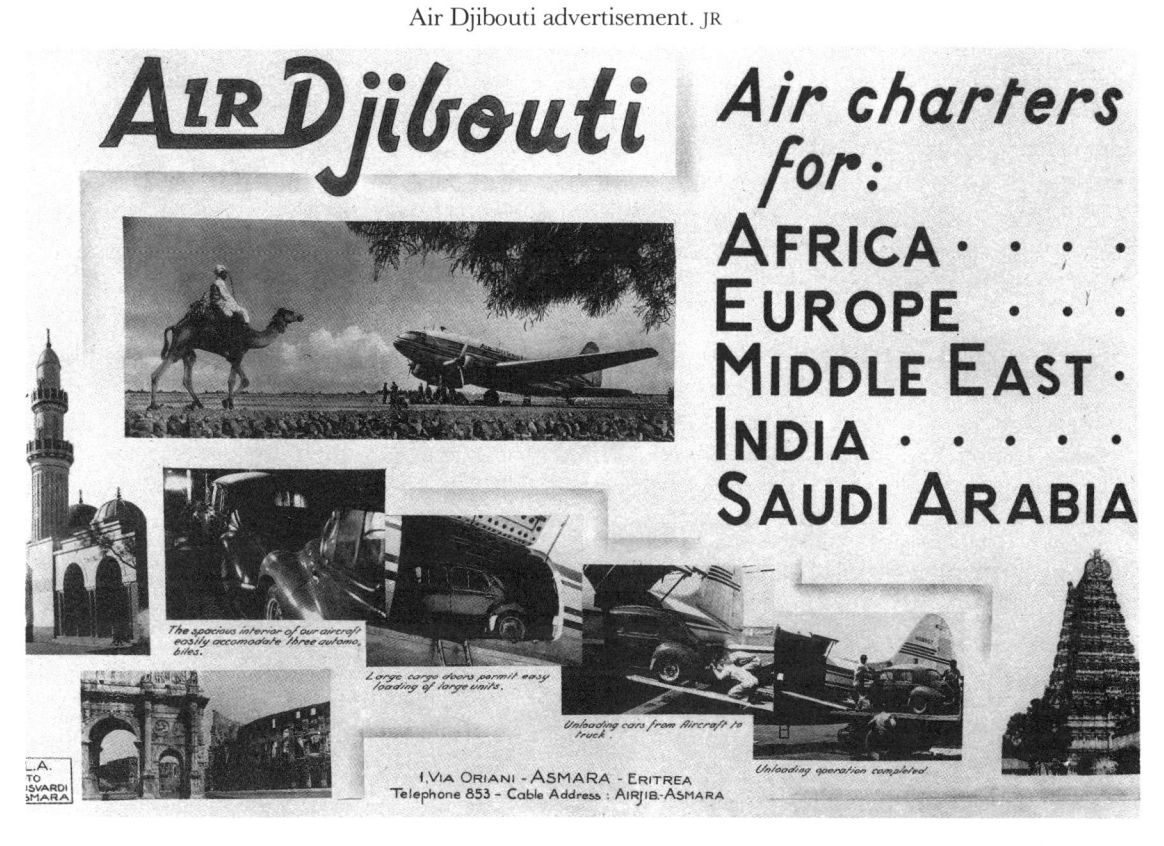

Celebrating new DC-3 flight schedule from Amman, Jordan to Cairo, Egypt, in front of the Shepherd Hotel in Cairo. Top row left: TAL's John Russell, bottom row, second from left: TAL's Ed Ringo, others unidentified. JR

operating in Amman. Afghanistan, where we had established our hajj movements, had been ruled out because of its isolation.

"Nelson was extremely interested in the possibility of having a scheduled carrier in the Middle East since Transocean planes carrying the Air Jordan flag would give the airline easy access to other Middle East countries. This tilted the decision in favor of owner Pasha Bilbeisi's Air Jordan.

"We would use some of Air Djibouti's personnel and as many Arab-speaking employees as possible. Supplies and equipment came from Lebanon, and customs duty had to be paid on supplies shipped into Jordan. As a result, we performed our maintenance in Beirut and kept our offices there, along with other facets of TAL operations that included the export/import division."

Later, Munther Bey Bilbeisi, son of the Pasha, opened a trading office for TAL in Baghdad, capital of Iraq, on the banks of the Tigris River, where merchants in the old covered bazaars traded in carpets, wool, hides, dates, tea, and cotton.

In December 1951 Libya attained its independence as a constitutional monarchy after years of rule by Italy and after the end of World War II by a British mandate. This north African desert country with a coastline on the Mediterranean Sea is inhabited mainly by wandering Bedouin tribesmen. In the extreme south live the veiled Tauregs. Air Jordan was called upon by Libya for assistance in its race to develop its oil fields. Its services were used by Mobiloil of Canada, Continental Oil Company, Caltex, Standard Oil of Indiana, and Robert Ray Geophysics, Inc., in addition to ARAMCO.

Scheduled flights by Air Jordan provided supplies and services to the desert oil camps. In addition to the cargo, Air Jordan carried oil crews who were given one-week furloughs in Tripoli or Benghazi at the end of every four weeks of work in the desert.

The effect of Air Djibouti and Air Jordan's presence on the oil exploration program was incalculable. Work which would have taken months without Air Jordan's wings took days or weeks. Delays due to equipment breakdown were minimal. Even when no flight was scheduled on the day of an emergency in the oil fields, Air Jordan would rush a special flight, and the needed parts or supplies would arrive in hours.

Operating aircraft in the severe weather and desert terrain of the Middle East was charged with problems unique to the area. The solutions frequently required the most inventive efforts of TAL's ground and flight crews.

A freak accident with no known cause once occurred on the ramp at Jeddah. The starboard wing of TAL's 967 exploded. A replacement was shipped from California but was destroyed when it was dropped while being offloaded on the Jeddah docks. (Transocean's Tommy Walker's screams could be heard all the way to Beirut, 883 miles away). A second replacement wing was discovered in Cairo and purchased from the Egyptian Air Force. TAL stripped and modified it for transit, then hung it under the fuselage of TAL 966 in a specially built cradle for the flight to Jeddah.

Refueling in Zahedan, Iran, always presented exceptional problems for the pilots. They first had

TAL-built cradle for aircraft wing being ferried from Cairo, Egypt to Jeddah, Saudi Arabia on C-46 aircraft. JR

to circle the tower to signal the gas truck to be ready to refuel. Then they had to go around and buzz the field to disperse camels from the runway in order to land. One unlucky pilot hit a fence while landing and had to remove the 200 feet of barbed wire wrapped around the tail wheel.

Publicity for Transocean Air Lines often took creative turns as well. For example, Transocean's Dave Gregory capitalized on the fact that the air route from Cairo to Jerusalem passed over the Dead Sea at 1000 feet below sea level. Dave founded the "Below Sea Level Flying Club."

Several hundred bright yellow membership cards were printed with the Air Jordan logo which certified that the card holder was a qualified member of the exclusive club and had the right to ask: "How low can you get . . . and still fly?"

The club's cards were the topic of conversation among flight crews and seasoned travelers of other airlines transiting the Middle East. Surprisingly, this club generated considerable business for Air Jordan.

Fierce competition from Arab Airways and Middle East Air Line kept Air Jordan's managers scrambling to maintain profitability. Two events during each year gave Air Jordan its greatest income: the hajj (the pilgrimage to Mecca), and flying U.S. Navy personnel on vacation from Beirut to Jerusalem whenever the Sixth Fleet was visiting Beirut. It was Stan Kochenderfer, Roland Swanson, and others of TAL's Middle East offices who effectively cut the competition to zero. They went directly to U.S. Naval Headquarters at Barcelona and won for Transocean the contract for all of the Navy's tour business before the fleet's departure for Beirut.

Air Djibouti. Packing gasoline up a ladder by hand so it can be funneled into the wing tank, Kandahar, Afghanistan. RL

Ethiopian Air Lines DC-3, ready to receive gasoline, Port Sudan, Africa. RL

Air Jordan C-46F, 44-78655, ex N-1668M, Taloa paint scheme. Photo taken at TAL's Hangar 28, Oakland Municipal Airport, Oakland, California. WTL

Left to right: Pasha Bilbeisi of Air Jordan, TAL's John Russell, Pasha's assistant, TAL Captain John Waterman, TAL Vice President S.L. Wilson. RL

Japan

By 1950, Transocean was prominent in the Orient, and Nelson finally had his chance to set up the first operation of a scheduled Japanese airline during October of 1951. TAL's operation was established under an agreement with Northwest Airlines, which had been awarded the original contract by the Japanese. But at the time, Northwest was unable to furnish the equipment and crews, and Transocean had both. Therefore, TAL was given a subcontract and started the service with four Martin 202s and in February of 1952, flew out two more Northwest airplanes to supplement the operation. The flights linked the main island of Honshu with the industrial centers on the other islands and the Martins carried about 80 percent load capacity.

On October 23, 1952, the corporation entered into a contract with Japan Air Lines whereby TAL would furnish all flight crew personnel and dispatchers, plus seven instructors, under the direction of Gene Cohan, Director of Far East Operations for Transocean, to train crews for the JAL domestic routes. Among the station managers at JAL were Dick Laskelle and Larry Bovat, with Dispatcher Vic Lakin. The contract also called for a maintenance facility, Japan Air Lines Maintenance Company (JAMCO) to be established, with mechanics and instructors to be supplied by Transocean. Within the year, TAL also furnished flight crews for JAL's international operation, with a minimum of twenty-four additional TAL flight crew members assigned to the operation.

On September 15, 1953, Captain Claude Turner, Japan Air Lines' chief pilot, delivered the first DC-6B to Japan to inaugurate JAL's international service on November 1, which would provide two flights a week between Tokyo and San Francisco.

TAL DC-4. Mt. Fuji, Japan in view. RL

Captain Robert Hench, Tokyo, Japan. RL

Left to right: Gene Cohan (TAL director of Far East operations), Mr. Toma (chief executive, Government of Ryukyus Islands), General Moore (commanding general, Rycom IX Corps), Mr. Nakamatsu (chief justice, Ryukyus Superior Court), Mr. Kamimura (deputy chief executive, Government of Ryukyus Islands), W.L. Keating (TAL vice president of operations), Tatabin Yogi (speaker, Ryukyus Legislature) and Mr. Honda. HGE

Afghanistan

Afghanistan was the next country to enlist the services of Transocean. The year was 1953. This mountainous country with a primitive transportation system relied heavily on small trucks and camel caravans to move goods over the Khyber Pass to and from distant markets. The government contracted for weekly TAL air service between Kabul and Cairo with intermediate stops at Kandahar and Jerusalem. Connections to Western Europe and the United States were made at Cairo, Egypt.

Iran

Iran was yet another country to benefit from Transocean's assistance. TAL first began operations there in 1948 by training Iranian Air Lines pilots and providing aircraft maintenance. In addition to flying the Moslem pilgrims to Jeddah, they often flew the Shahansha of Iran, His Imperial Majesty Mohammed Reza Shah Pahlavi on journeys to Rome, Geneva, Rabat, Formosa, Japan, or other destinations.

The first flight by the polar route from Oakland International Airport was made to deliver a TAL DC-4 to Iranian Air Lines in Teheran. The aircraft departed on January 7, 1955, with Orvis Nelson in command with a crew of six. On board were 8,000 pounds of cargo that included spare engines and arctic survival gear.

The first stop was at Duluth, Minnesota, for final clearances and special winterizing of the plane. There, de-icing gear and special fluids to resist the cold would be installed.

The polar route chosen by Nelson was similar to the one flown by Scandinavian Airlines Systems (SAS). It penetrated 200 miles north of the Arctic Circle which saved more than 400 miles on the 10,000 mile flight. The course took them within twenty miles of Bluie West 8, code name of a U.S. military air base in Greenland. Their next stop was Keflavik, Iceland. Then they proceeded to Beirut via Dusseldorf, Geneva, and Athens.

Germany

Less than ten years after the United States had been at war with Germany, the West German airline, Lufthansa, wanted to do business with TAL. It requested Transocean to supply navigators for its new transatlantic service. TAL provided ten navigators for the first year of operation. Pilots and engineers of Lufthansa had previously been trained at the

Iranair DC-4. DC-3 in background, Teheran, Iran. HGE

Taloa Academy of Aeronautics in Oakland.

As a collateral enterprise for the establishment and management of foreign airlines, TAL formed a purchasing organization to buy and export spare parts for foreign companies using American equipment. This developed into another lucrative business for the airline.

During its fourteen years of flying, Transocean crossed not only geographical borders to work with peoples and governments around the world, but also broke through the barriers of language, religion, and diverse backgrounds in its globe-encircling activities.

The skies knew no boundaries; neither did Transocean Air Lines.

Two TAL DC-4s at Oakland Municipal Airport, Oakland, California. Thousands of WWII refugees were transported to Venezuela; English, German and French war brides were flown to and from the USA. Support for the Berlin Airlift was also accomplished via these planes. N79992 shown in the foreground. RL

Transocean Flies Around the World

Saudi Arabian Air Line aircraft. General Ibrahim Tassan, director general of Civil Aviation of the Kingdom of Saudi Arabia accepts the first of five aircraft purchased from Transocean Air Lines, Idlewild Airport, New York. Left to right: General Tassan, Captain Frank Kendall, E.W. Ringo and Orvis Nelson. EI

Conference, Saudi Arabian style. RL

Orvis Nelson, second from right, at conference in Saudi Arabia. RL

No Tow? No Problem! Everybody Push! Saudi Arabia, 1952. RL

Saudi Arabia Airline

King Ibn Saud of Saudi Arabia arrives to test elevator on his Flying Palace, (SAR-4), 1952. RL

SAR-4 arrives Jeddah, September 1952. King Ibn Saud at top of stairs. RL

Ed Peiffer. EP

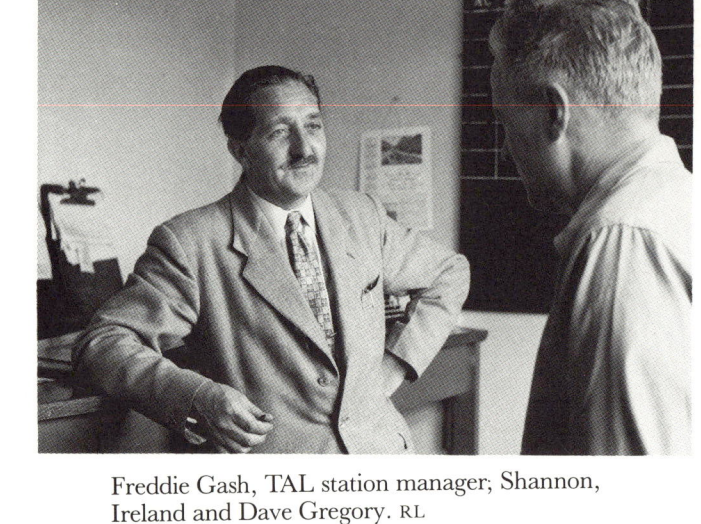
Freddie Gash, TAL station manager; Shannon, Ireland and Dave Gregory. RL

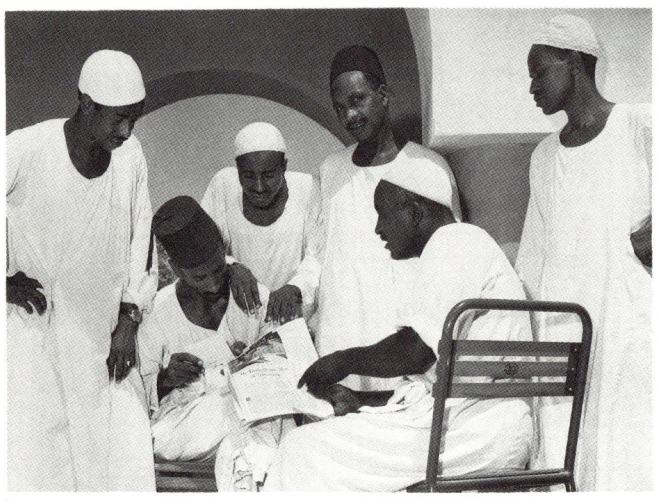
Looking over *Saturday Evening Post* article about TAL, titled "The Daring Young Men of Transocean," Africa. 1952. RL

Strolling through Rome, Italy. Left to right: Robert Judd, Everett Mendenhall, unidentified Philippine Air Lines' purser, Pacita Magtoto, Bill Leonard, Mr. Buenaventura, purser. RL

A Transocean loading crew stows baggage aboard the "Taloa Shanghai" in Honolulu, Hawaii. RL

S.A. Nichols and Ed Hogan with friends in the Middle East. HGE

Chapter Three: The Daring Young Flight Crews
...and Their Flying Machines

"Flying: Hours of boredom interrupted by moments of sheer terror."

CAPTAIN TED VINSON and his crew left Wake Island on a routine flight to Guam on May 12, 1950. Sixteen construction workers were in the rear of the DC-4 and a load of cargo was tied down in the front of the cabin.

Engine number one began to run rough about two hours out. Vinson feathered it and radioed TAL at Wake Island that he was heading back to the base. Before many minutes had passed, engine number two blew an oil line and was also feathered. The aircraft immediately began to lose altitude. Vinson called Purser John Foster up front and directed him to inform the passengers of the emergency and that the rear door would be jettisoned in an attempt to lighten the load.

Next, Foster grabbed a hatchet and cut the cargo ropes. He then tied a rope around his waist and secured the other end to the bottom of a seat frame before he and some of the passengers began throwing cargo out the door.

Just as he reported back to Vinson, engine number four quit.

"Son, you'd better make this airplane lighter or we're all going for a swim."

"You mean jettison everything?"

"Get everything out of this goddamned airplane that you can get out!"

Foster hurried to follow orders while Vinson broadcast a Mayday. Then Vinson managed to restart engine number one, although it was still out of synchronization.

The plane continued losing altitude as Foster alternated between jettisoning additional cargo and dashing to the cockpit to ask, "Is it light enough yet?"

"Keep throwin', keep throwin' — get it lighter or we're goin' in the drink!"

The frantic purser and the passengers tossed out everything they could get their hands on: the sextant, crew baggage, all the seats, the upholstery, the honey buckets (toilets), and even the navigator's shoes.

By the time the Air-Sea Rescue ship arrived on the scene, Vinson was flying at an altitude of only 500 feet. He managed to keep the DC-4 at that altitude by holding full opposite rudder to avoid going into a spin.

Soon, another Transocean aircraft arrived from Wake. Unable to fly alongside because he would stall if he attempted the same slow airspeed as the crippled ship, the pilot of the second airplane had to fly lazy circles around it.

Captain Vinson and co-pilot Floyd Calvin, escorted by the second TAL plane, nursed the airliner back to Wake, shirts and undershorts dangling from its tail. Everyone on the island had awaited word of its fate, and the group waiting on the tarmac sent up a rousing cheer as the plane touched the runway.

The TAL operations and sales departments, and dispatchers such as Ray Foster, Bill Wilson, Lou Lombard, Stu Seuberth, John Willhalm, Don Sheets and Les Forden were often hard-pressed to keep track of Transocean's airplanes. The crew of one DC-4 might be flying Chinese Nationalist refugees to Latin America, another transporting a shipload of Catholic "Holy Year" pilgrims to Rome, while thousands of monkeys were en route via Transocean from India to the United States where they would be used in the research program of Dr. Jonas Salk to develop a polio vaccine.

Adventure in Brazil

On at least two occasions Transocean aircraft and crews simply disappeared. What should have been a routine flight to South America in November 1949, for example, became a five day ordeal for Transocean's Captain Harvey Rogers, his crew, and forty-five Russian immigrants being transported to Asuncion, Paraguay.

Herman Humm flew as first officer; Roy Minson, third pilot; John Hoenninger, navigator; Charley Bradley, engineer; Tommy Sconce, radioman; Ed Hovlid, purser; and Vi Corrington, R.N., stewardess.

The first leg of the flight was from Oakland to Panama where they stayed overnight before heading for Lima, Peru, the next morning. Hoenninger brought from Oakland all the required flight maps and charts but had been unable to obtain additional information about Asunción and the routes used by other airlines prior to departure time. The crew was therefore unaware that the Asunción station required a service fee to be paid in advance.

The flight left for Lima on the morning of November 23 in clear weather, crossing the Andes and the Bolivian *altiplano* near La Paz and Cochabamba before turning south. Below, the vast jungles of Brazil appeared to be one great sea of green trees. No rivers or other landmarks were visible to the crew.

Omminous appearing storm clouds were brewing over the area by the time the aircraft neared Asunción several hours later. So Rogers descended below the clouds to fly visual flight rules (VFR) over the flat and rolling terrain below. Locating the airport using radio aids would have been easy, but the radio beacons were not turned on.

Rogers circled in the clear, waiting while Hoenninger tried to get a sunline to plot a navigation fix on his chart. This proved impossible. One minute a patch of sunshine would appear, then heavy, black clouds would roll in to block the sun. When the aircraft began to be lashed by torrential rains, Rogers had no choice but to climb above the weather and head for Rio de Janeiro, the first alternate airport.

Everybody in the cockpit was tense, wondering if they could make it to Rio de Janeiro through the storm before the gasoline ran out. In the meantime, Sconce kept busy changing radio frequencies in an effort to raise somebody. The static proved to be so fierce that it was impossible for him to get a response.

Then, just before sunset, the DC-4 passed over a large river they determined to be the Parana. Minutes later, Rogers spotted a small dirt and grass airstrip in the midst of the jungle that may have been used at one time by the mining companies or coffee plantations in the area. A windsock fluttered in the wind at one end of the field. There were no buildings in sight nor any lights—just a primitive jungle landing strip.

Rogers took a vote from the crew as to whether they should attempt to land or take a chance on reaching Rio. Because they were unsure of their exact location and as it would soon be dark and the fuel supply was now dangerously low, the vote was unanimous to land.

Rogers reduced the power and dropped altitude quickly to survey the field to see if he would be able to land safely on the dirt strip. He decided there was enough room, though barely, and made what Roy Minson terms an excellent "drag in" approach at slow speed, and landed as close to the end of the field as the trees would allow.

"It was a beautiful landing," said Minson. "We hit the earth softly and used only half the length of the field, or about 1,500 feet. And all of us were amazed at how rapidly the plane slowed to a stop.

"We later discovered that we'd landed on sand and that the wheels had dropped in about six inches making the drag terrific which was just what we needed. We were safe in Paranavai, Brazil, a little wooden-hut city at the edge of coffee country."

It was dusk when the crew put down the ladder and descended into a crowd of several hundred native Indians.

In an effort to get a fix on their location, Hoenninger showed a few of the men a chart, attempting sign language to try to make them understand what he wanted. Each Indian pointed to a different place on the chart, so Hoenninger decided to wait until dark, then board the aircraft and take star shots. He was then able to determine that they were at what apparently was "Lovatt."

The natives whooped in delight when he spoke the word to them, just as if they knew what he meant. But there was no "Lovatt" on the map.

Finally, as if to "show him a thing or two," the Indians led the navigator to a tiny radio shack set back amongst the trees and pulled out an old and very dusty chart.

The longitude shown on the chart didn't make any sense at all until Hoenninger recalled that longitude might depend on the country. The map proved to be perfect when Rio de Janeiro was considered zero meridian. "Lovatt" was, in fact, Mandaguari, a city some sixty miles from Paranavai.

Sconce fired up one of the engines every day to generate enough electricity to send radio transmissions to get help and to attempt to notify TAL's headquarters at Oakland Municipal of their whereabouts. Hordes of Indians would run from behind the airplane into the slipstream, throwing themselves flat, laughing and hollering, trying to see who could come closest to the propeller until the crew put a stop to the dangerous game.

The mayor's wife provided platters of fruit, chicken, partridge and other meats, and graciously offered their hut for lodging. However, the passengers and most of the crew stayed nearby in a small hotel.

In the meantime, officials of the government of Brazil had heard Sconce's radio transmissions and directed several busses to Paranavai to move the passengers and most of the crew to the airport at Mandaguari. This was necessary because the DC-4 could not have taken off from the small landing strip with so much weight on board. To lighten the load even more, four of the seats were also removed. The passengers and baggage would later be picked up by Rogers at Mandaguari.

Rogers taxied the plane into position at the grassy end of the strip where the surface was solid. No one knew what to expect when the wheels hit the sand. He then set the brakes and revved the engines to full power before releasing the brakes.

"I had never seen a DC-4 accelerate so fast," said Minson. "With flaps partially down, it slowed only momentarily on the sand before popping into the air with nothing to spare. I'm sure there were tree branches in the wheels, but ol' Harv really pulled one off that time.

"Looking back, it actually was impossible to fly a DC-4 out of that short field at Paranavai," he said. "But at Transocean we always believed we could accomplish the impossible, and usually did, so it never even occured to us that we couldn't. We just went ahead and did it."

The trip had already proved highly adventurous, but there were still some surprises in store for the crew members. For starters, they had been told only that the airport at Mandaguari was large and had two runways. No mention had been made that the runways were perched on top of a hill. This required Rogers to first fly down into the valley, then up to the airfield to land uphill. Under the conditions, this was the only approach possible.

When they arrived, Rogers circled the field and chose the runway most into the wind. The end of the runway on Roger's approach was seventy-five feet below the middle of the strip, while the other end was only slightly downhill from the middle. It was like landing on an arch, and Rogers made a perfect touchdown.

The last 250 gallons of fuel remaining in the tanks of the DC-4 had been used en route from Paranavai. So upon their arrival in Mandaguari, the Brazilian Air Force allowed the crew to borrow 1,000 gallons of gas, which was just enough to fly half the passengers to Curitiba, about 250 miles away. This was done to ensure that the plane would return to pick up the rest of the passengers. Later, at Curitiba, the auxiliary tanks were filled with replacement fuel.

Shortly after their arrival at Mandaguari, something extraordinary happened that the Transocean crew members would never forget.

Rumors that Hitler was still alive and possibly in South America were prevalent in 1949. And shortly after the arrival of the Transocean plane at Mandaguari, questions were raised in the minds of the crew as to the truth behind these rumors.

Out of the jungle came a calvacade of shiny, automobiles and limousines, rolling along single file and manned by impeccably dressed, obviously wealthy Germans who spoke English fluently.

They invited the American crew members to join them for dinner and ushered them into the waiting cars. Twenty minutes later they came to a beautiful clearing in the middle of the jungle where an impressive lodge stood near a meandering brook. The tables in the dining room of the lodge were set with fine china and held a lavish display of food. There was also a bar where every conceivable type of drink was available.

Hoenninger said that there were at least twenty-five Germans at the banquet and that they asked many questions of the crew: How did you know where we were? Are you surprised to find us here? Did you come to bomb us?

He and the others thought it highly unusual for the colony to be hidden in the middle of a nearly impenetrable rain forest, living in homes set back among the trees surrounding the lodge. After all, they could have chosen to live in Rio de Janeiro or some other large South American city.

Just what kind of refugees were these people, they asked each other later. Were they loyal to Hitler? If so, how did they escape from Germany? Was Hitler really dead? Or was he there? Who were these Germans? The crew was never able to find out who the mysterious people were, or why they chose to live in the Brazilian jungle, although John Hoenninger reportedly tried for some time to find answers to these provocative questions.

At least two more incidents around that time seemed to indicate a conspiracy against Transocean in South America. One of these occurred when Panagra advised all the American Society of Travel

Agents (ASTA) and the International Air Transport Association (IATA) travel agents in Latin America that Panagra would cancel their agency agreements and put them out of business if they sold any Transocean Air Lines' tickets. The other was when Braniff refused to lend or provide for a ramp—even with pay—to discharge one of TAL's planeloads of passengers at Tocuman (Panama) Airport. "Find a rope and shinny down," reportedly was Braniff's reply.

Holy War

Nothing was neutral about Transocean, it seemed, except perhaps its stance of neutrality in the Arab-Jewish situation that existed in 1948. Despite this fact, their international relations were sometimes complicated by unusual circumstances.

In August of 1948, Transocean contracted with the International Refugee Organization (IRO) for a flight from Paris to Australia with fifty European refugees. The flight plan was complicated because some of the passengers were Jews. This meant that TAL would be unable to take the most direct route and would need to avoid flying over any Arabian countries. The plan called for the aircraft to be routed from Paris over Rome and Athens with the first refueling stop to be Abadan, Iran.

Before take off, Captain Galvin "Ace" Sargent was handed a cablegram ostensibly from TAL's office in Shannon, Ireland. Its instructions were for him to continue past Abadan and land at Dhahran, Saudi Arabia on the Persian Gulf. The message was received without any suspicion, and Sargent insisted that a confirmation of the new plan had been made en route over Paris.

Before the transport's descent over Saudi Arabia and landing at Dhahran, the uneventful flight was forced to deviate from the flight plan. The traffic control tower at Dhahran refused permission to land.

In the middle of the Arab world, carrying a charter of Jews, and now low on fuel, the situation looked bleak. Why was the flight plan changed by Shannon and now permission to land denied? wondered Sargent.

After many airports in the Persian Gulf refused landing rights to Captain Sargent, the Iraqis across the Gulf at Basra finally granted permission. The tower cleared aircraft to land and refuel.

When it came to a stop near the terminal, it was rushed by soldiers carrying rifles. Even with the propellers still rotating and the cabin door still closed, the crew on deck knew they were hostages in the hands of angry adversaries.

The stairs were rolled into place against the fuselage, and the door opened. The armed guards took physical control of all flight personnel and passengers as well as the aircraft. Bob Glattly, who was the TAL navigator, said that the soldiers threatened to kill everyone as they herded them into a hotel at the airport. It was then that the crew realized the unfortunate political significance of landing Jews in an Arab country.

Now out of radio contact with the world, the Transocean flight was reported as lost and unaccounted for. Immediately, Transocean at Oakland, with the aid of the U.S. government and her allies, tried to solve the mystery of the disappearance of Captain Sargent's plane. Three days later, a pilot flying for an oil company landed at the airport and saw the Transocean plane. After his departure, he reported its location on the ramp at Basra to the airline's Middle East division offices.

Orvis Nelson always believed that this incident was created by a nationalistic or communistic group intent on stirring up international strife. The U.S. State Department, the IRO, and Transocean headquarters negotiated for eighteen days before the aircraft and its passengers were allowed to continue to the destination, Australia.

While it seemed Transocean's fate to fight for everything from route certificates to ramp space, to rescuing its own aircraft, these incidents merely served to highlight the company's ingenuity and corporate vitality.

Orvis' Orient Express

The largest, most daring, ferry operation ever undertaken by a civilian airline was accomplished by Transocean flight crews and maintenance men during the spring of 1948. It began when the Chinese Nationalist Air Force purchased 150 Curtiss C-46 twin-engined aircraft from the U.S. government and asked Transocean to bid on the "de-mothballing" of the stored surplus aircraft, the overhauling of the planes and the engines, and their delivery to Shanghai, China. They were to be used by General Chiang Kai-shek's air force.

Transocean lost the contract for the overhauling of the engines but presented such a daring and ingenious plan for the transfer of the airplanes to Shanghai that Nelson and his associates won the ferrying contract.

Transocean's idea for solving the transportation problem was to fit the C-46 Commandos with

Chinese Army aircraft #C46289, one of 150 Curtiss C-46Ds TAL ferried to Shanghai, China, 1948. WTL

auxiliary long-range fuel tanks and fly them across the Pacific to China. All the other bidders had insisted on dismantling the overhauled aircraft and shipping them across the Pacific by steamship.

Heavy odds were placed against the success of TAL's projected sky ferry operation (experts estimated a loss of at least ten aircraft). But this was exactly the sort of challenge that Nelson and his staff enjoyed.

The special cabin tanks to extend the range from 1,500 to 2,600 miles were installed in each C-46 at Transocean's Oakland maintenance base. Then test flights were made to determine the fuel consumption of the modified transports.

Detailed arrangements were then made to station mechanics at the Pacific island bases on the route. At these intermediate points would be spare parts, engines, and fuel.

The flight plan called for a zigzag route originating in Los Angeles, then to Oakland, and on to Honolulu, Wake, Guam, Okinawa, and finally to Shanghai. The C-46s were dispatched in groups of five, and a Transocean DC-4 was flown to China to bring the crews back to Oakland.

Transocean safely ferried all 150 of the C-46s. They logged over a million and a half miles over the Pacific Ocean en route to China. There was only one incident. The 148th Commando lost an engine four hundred miles offshore from Oakland but returned on its remaining engine for repairs before completing the trip.

Later, Transocean flight crews also ferried a fleet of Grumman Albatrosses across the Pacific without incident in a contract operation involving more than 1,000,000 miles of flying. The flying boats were delivered from the factory at Bethpage, on Long Island, New York, to Jakarta for the Indonesian Supply Mission.

Transocean's pilots were modern day swashbucklers. Young and daring, most were in their twenties, yet they were tough and capable, with a professionalism unequaled by their contemporaries of the scheduled airlines. Most had been seasoned by war. They took on any challenge, blazed new air routes, sometimes landing where no other large aircraft had been, and set speed records as a matter of course. For example, late in 1958, a TAL Super Constellation on a contract cargo flight from Tokyo landed at Oakland more than eleven hours ahead of schedule, with a little help from the jetstream during a portion of the transpacific hop. Captain Jesse Morrison logged the one-stop flight of approximately 5,500 miles at fifteen hours and twenty-two minutes.

The $75,000 Brown Paper Sack

A most unforgettable TAL captain was Ran Reid, a transplanted Texan known for his dry sense of humor. Reid had been flying construction workers between Guam and Manila during the fall of 1948. On November 7, just as he prepared to leave the blocks at Guam to return to Oakland, the station manager ran out to hand the purser a paper sack he said contained $75,000. The money was to be delivered to Oakland for the November 10 payroll.

During climb-out from Guam, the purser insisted that Reid be the one to take the money to Oakland, but as there was no paper work to go with it, and because he hadn't counted it, Captain Reid told the purser to take the responsibility and deliver the money himself.

"During our three-day layover in Honolulu, the purser ate and slept with that paper sack, still not opening it or counting the money," said Reid. "No one wanted to associate with him because of that large amount of cash, so he must've figured it to be a bag full of trouble. During our flight from Honolulu to Oakland, unknown to any of us, the purser threw the sack behind the reserve oil tank under the lower bunk, and on our arrival at Oakland at 4 a.m., he left the plane in a hurry.

"Well, after a thirteen hour flight, I didn't feel like filling out my expense report to account for my $1,500 advance, which was all spent but $22 anyhow, so I headed home to go to bed.

"I'd just gone to sleep when Sherwood Nichols banged on the front door. He said he was sorry to have to wake me but, ahem, he needed that money to meet the payroll. Well, I got hot under the collar and told him it was all gone but $22. Then, when I saw his face go pale and his jaw drop about nine inches, I hollered, 'well, my crew had to eat, you know!'

"Nichols then realized that we were talking about two different bags of money. I was referring to my expense money, and he was looking for the $75,000. I told him that the purser had it, and should have turned it in. And Nichols headed back to the field.

"Well, in the meantime a maintenance man had removed the auxiliary oil tank, found the paper sack and, thinking it was somebody's lunch, put it on a desk, but no one knew that at the time.

"The purser couldn't be located until twelve hours later, so it was eight o'clock that night before the paper sack was tracked down and someone from the payroll department sent to the hangar to retrieve it. The entire $75,000 was present and accounted for."

On a Wing and a Prayer

Weather often played a dramatic role in Transocean's around-the-world operation as reporting aids were few and unsophisticated during the forties and fifties. One incident in which weather played havoc with a TAL aircraft occurred in 1957 when a DC-4 was en route to Tokyo carrying a passenger load of fifty-three Catholic nuns. The crew were briefed by the meterological office on Wake Island that a severe typhoon was about to pass through the Tokyo area shortly before their ETA (estimated time of arrival). However, they were assured that the storm would be fifty miles northeast of Haneda International by the time they landed.

On their arrival at 1:30 in the morning, they found themselves in the middle of the typhoon, which had taken out all the lights in the vicinity of the airport and disrupted ground communications as well.

Unable to land, the pilot flew the aircraft, for over an hour in severe turbulence, in an eliptical holding pattern on the Kisarazu homer just off the Japanese coast.

Radio Operator Ralph Lewis remembers the storm as the worst he experienced during his flying career. "Suddenly, it felt as though we had struck a brick wall. The plane shot up a thousand feet, climbing at the rate of 2,000 feet a minute, with all four engines throttled back.

"Then without warning, we hit the ceiling and began to fall, fluttering down like a leaf in a breeze, again at 2,000 feet a minute with full throttle applied. My work table was thrown to the floor, and I was oscillating between the floor and the ceiling.

"Before long, a torrent of rain began leaking through the windshield. The two pilots were getting soaked, and I remember them yelling over the din for towels.

"To add to the excitement, a phenomenon seen during electrical storms and known as Saint Elmo's Fire was shooting long fingers of blue light in front of the four propeller blades.

"Lightning struck the aircraft with loud explosions. And it sounded like someone was outside beating on the fuselage with a baseball bat.

"When the storm subsided, we picked up the cockpit debris, then worked our way back to the passenger cabin, where the nuns were all over the place. Fortunately, no one was severely injured.

"After a half-hour of circling, the runway and airport lights were restored, and we landed in a gusty forty-mile-an-hour crosswind. There were at least three inches of water on the runway, and because the heavy winds would have blown the boarding ramp (stairs) over, we were forced to stay on board the aircraft. But no one cared. We slept in our seats until daylight, thankful that we were safe on the ground. I still think it was the fervent 'Hail Marys' offered up by those fifty-three women that brought us through."

Transocean Goes Hollywood

In 1953, Transocean Air Lines assisted Hollywood in making two movies, both based on novels written by Ernest K. Gann who was a pilot for TAL at the time. Gann's own experience with TAL provided much of the background used in the books.

"Island In The Sky," which starred John Wayne, is the dramatic story of a search for the crew of an Army Air Force transport which had been forced to land in the wilds of Labrador after becoming lost in a bitter snowstorm. The downed pilot and his crew were employees of an airline assigned to the Air Transport Command during World War II, as were the pilots and crew members of the Douglas C-47s in the search party.

Said author Gann of the book, "This is not a war story. It could have been written at any time since man took to the air. This is the story about professional pilots and their special, guarded world—their island in the sky. The men in the story are fictitious characters, but their counterparts can be found in cockpits all over the world. Now they are flying at war. Tomorrow they will be flying at peace. For regardless of the world's condition, flying is their life."

Late in 1952, Bill Benge was commissioned by Director Bill Wellman to lease three DC-3s for the movie from Trans World Airlines (TWA).

By the middle of January 1953 the first flying scenes were filmed in the middle of a snowstorm at Donner Lake in the Sierra Nevada mountains of California. A camera crew flew in another airplane alongside as the three Transocean flight crews took the DC-3s in low over the mountain tops. Two of TAL's aircraft mechanics were along to assist in making over one of the DC-3s to appear to be a crashed aircraft.

Much of the actual flying for this movie was done by TAL flight captains Bill Benge and Bill Word under the technical supervision of Gann. Captains Robert Bunbury and Francis Kennedy also assisted, along with copilots Shelby Pitts, William Tieman, Jack Elsbree, and Charles Hallman.

Douglas Aircraft Company's Chief Pilot Johnny Martin said that the film had some of the best flying in it he'd ever seen. Director Wellman agreed and gave each member of Transocean's flight crews and the two mechanics a bonus of $1,000 each for what he called superior flying.

In November 1953, "The High and The Mighty" was filmed with Transocean providing technical advice, pilots to fly the airplanes, and mechanics to accomplish the job of installing the drooping engine called for in the script.

The $2 million production starred John Wayne with actors Robert Stack and Phil Harris, and actresses Claire Trevor, Laraine Day, and Jan Sterling. The film's characters were on board a flight from Hawaii to the mainland, little dreaming of the trouble in store for them. The aerial photography was accomplished in two TAL DC-4s flown by Captains Bill Keating and Bill Benge, with Benge also serving as technical advisor.

Benge spent two weeks working with Wellman's special effects department preparing for the cockpit scene and building removable doors on both sides of the plane's fuselage so that either side could be removed for filming.

The movie, which was only the fourth picture to be made in cinemascope and color, was shot at various locations. The departure scene was made at the Flying Tigers hangar at Burbank, California, supposedly Honolulu; the scene depicting an engine fire was filmed at the airport at Glendale, California. The design for tilting the "fire damaged" engine at a 30-degree angle, as called for in the script, was produced by Al Macedo, Transocean's chief engineer and accomplished by Hangar 28 mechanics. They also blacked out the propeller with paint so it wouldn't show in the movie. When they were in the process of changing the "damaged" engine, a large amount of oil was accidentally dropped onto the side of the cowling. The effect of the oil spill on the reattached engine caused the make-believe damage to look authentic. "Wellman thought we were the greatest artists in the world," said Bill Benge, "and it was all due to a screw-up!"

TAL mechanics had installed the engine in the record time of three hours. When the filming was completed at midnight, the men reinstalled the engine in three more hours. Transocean's plane made its film debut, and in less than eight hours was back in service.

The movie company moved to the Oakland-

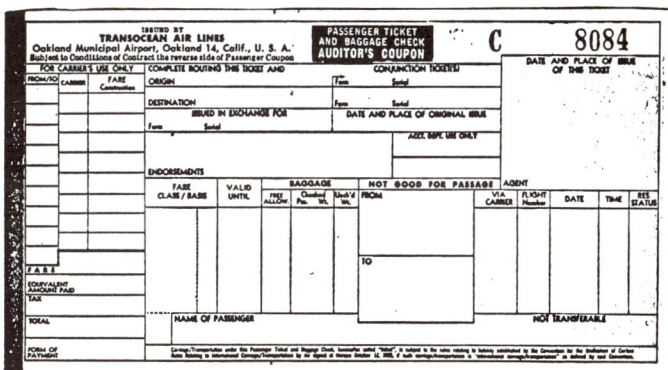

San Francisco area for the final landing scene at San Francisco Airport. Runway 28 Right was closed for one night while photographic shots were being taken on the ground and in the air for the landing scene. Fire trucks sprayed large amounts of water on the approach of the aircraft to make it appear that it was a rainy night. During the filming of this sequence Director Wellman kept ordering Keating to take the DC-4 lower and lower during a series of landings in an attempt to get the best shots. Keating came in low enough to wipe out five rows of approach lights before Wellman was finally satisfied. Transocean received a bill for eight hundred dollars for the damaged lights; Wellman picked up the tab.

"The High and The Mighty" was one of the most successful films of the fifties. It grossed over ten million dollars during the first three years after its release.

Yet another movie, "Julie," which starred Doris Day and Louis Jourdan, was filmed at The Taloa Academy of Aeronautics, and the San Francisco Airport. The plot of the suspense story centered on Louis Jourdan as a concert pianist who plans to murder his wife, played by Doris Day, who eventually has to assume control of the airplane on which they are flying. Both outdoor and indoor (simulator) shots were taken on Transocean's premise. TAL captains Bill Keating and Royal Minson instructed Doris Day how to handle the simulator controls properly. The camera was positioned behind the simulator, and its windshield was removed so that the filming would pick up a "process" screen in front of the simulator. This "process" screen would show all of the aerial views of snow-capped mountains and valleys so it appeared that she was actually flying an airplane.

For filming the landing scene, a large Mitchell camera was mounted in the co-pilot's seat of one of TAL's DC-4s to record the approach through the windshield of the aircraft. To achieve as much reality as possible, the director wanted the landing to appear rough — as though a novice was at the controls. But the pro at the controls was Captain Keating. "I kept the airspeed rather high because we would intentionally bounce the aircraft at least five or six times down the runway for interior and ground cameras. As a result of the long, fast approach and those bounces — which were between thirty and forty feet high into the air — when we turned off at the end of the runway, the outboard right tire blew out. We couldn't have done better if we'd tried!"

Movie star Doris Day, Holly Nelson and Orvis Nelson. Photo taken when "Julie" was being filmed at Taloa Academy, Oakland, California, 1956. RL

The design for tilting the "fire damaged" engine at a 30 degree angle for the movie, "The High and the Mighty" was produced by TAL's chief engineer Al Macedo, and installed by TAL mechanics Earl Jones, Stewart Taylor and Jack Richardson. 1953. TN

Movie stars Doris Day and Anne Robinson. Photo taken during scene from movie, "Julie," filmed at Taloa Academy, Oakland, California, 1956. BE

Cameraman and movie director Bill Wellman. Taken during filming of "The High and the Mighty" at TAL facility. HGE

"Yes, Indeed!"

Two of Transocean's Convair 240s were leased to fly the eighty performers of "The Show of Stars of 1952" to some fourteen one-night stands in the U.S. and Canada. Captains Ed Landwehr and Joe Goeller were with the group for three weeks, with Landwehr flying most of the troupe, and Goeller the musical instruments and some of the passengers. But the first flight left Memphis en route to Kansas City, Kansas, without Fats Domino (early rock 'n roll performer), who didn't like to fly and drove his white Cadillac to Kansas City. Once there, however, he was convinced by the other performers that flying with Transocean was "the greatest," and got aboard Landwehr's plane for the next leg of the journey. Fats became a believer. He was so thrilled with flying that he decided to buy a Convair for himself and his group. He asked Landwehr if he'd be his private pilot, but Landwehr declined, preferring to remain with the airline.

For a while, Transocean became a flying billboard for the Domino group. The titles of some Fats' most popular songs were painted on the nose of Captain Landwehr's plane, "I'm Walkin'," "Honky Tonk," "Yes, Indeed!," "Blueberry Hill," and other song titles greeted the thousands of teenagers who met the aircraft at every stop on the journey.

The Transocean Stork

While some of Transocean's flight crews were flying for the movies and others were getting their excitement out of risky foreign assignments, some were tending to "labor" problems in the sky.

The first of these incidents occurred during the summer of 1949 aboard a Transocean plane bound for New York from Germany filled with refugees, including two pregnant women. Both of the women's babies were due momentarily.

The flight from Munich became an ordeal for Captain Wally Kyse when both women went into labor en route to Prestwick, Scotland. Kyse took a five minute "correspondence course" in obstetrics by radio after sending a message to Prestwick: Two babies about to be born on my plane. What do I do?

The Prestwick controllers were momentarily baffled. The ground officer joked to Kyse that he'd better see whether the plane's motors had any more speed in them. They then called Dr. John Stevenson, the airport physician, who reduced midwifery to five easy steps—at least for Kyse. Fortunately, Kyse didn't have to apply the lesson. The infants cooperated by making their "landing" at a nearby hospital an hour after the plane touched down.

Captain Kyse's troubles may have been over, but the British immigration authorities were then faced with two new travelers without passports, and their mothers had no documents permitting them to stay in Scotland. Their husbands, also among the fifty-three passengers, were in the same situation. Several high-level conferences were required before the problem was resolved by sending the husbands on to New York, to be followed later by mothers and babes. Thus, an international problem was solved.

Captain Galvin "Ace" Sargent, who already had had enough trouble as a hostage in Basra, picked up all the extra speed he could when he also discovered three women in labor on one of his flights from Bremen, Germany, to Idlewild Airport in New York.

The first announcement that one of the women was having labor pains came from the purser when the aircraft was one hour from Meeks Bay, Iceland. Meeks Field was notified of the emergency, and an ambulance was waiting at the gate when the plane landed to whisk the mother-to-be to the local hospital.

In the air again, midway between Meeks Bay and Gander, Newfoundland, the purser reported to Captain Sargent another passenger was now in labor. Not only was she in extreme pain, but the birth seemed imminent.

Preparations were made in the crew compartment for the delivery. But once again, it was not needed as the aircraft touched down at Gander with minutes to spare.

Everybody sighed and relaxed as they anticipated an uneventful flight to New York. Nothing left to do now, thought Sargent, but fly the airplane.

Then, about an hour out of New York, the purser, who had aged considerably on this one transatlantic flight, reported to the captain that yet another woman was starting labor.

Believing that labor must be contagious, Sargent, who was by now thoroughly exasperated by this incredible string of blessed events, once more pushed the engines to the limit. For the third time, he managed to land moments before the baby arrived.

Captain Walt Lawton, however, didn't quite out-fly the stork. He lost the race by only a few minutes and a baby boy was born aboard the DC-4 that he and his crew were flying to Honolulu from Oakland (a twelve-hour flight) with a full load of tour group passengers. The two stewardesses were Alyce Martinez and Lori Mikosch, both of whom were single and in their early twenties.

Just before the plane reached the point of no return, Alyce called Lori aside.

"Lori, I think we've got a problem. There's a lady up front who's in labor."

"What?" What did you say?"

"She's going to have a baby!"

"That's impossible, Alyce."

"No it isn't, she's not feeling too good."

"You've got to be kidding. I don't remember seeing anyone who was pregnant."

"Well, she had on a full coat when she boarded so we didn't notice."

When Captain Lawton was notified of the emergency, he first determined that the woman wanted to proceed to Honolulu, instead of turning back to Oakland. He then radioed Honolulu for a doctor to give instructions. Meanwhile, the stewardesses put the woman in the crew bunk and made her as comfortable as possible. Messages from the doctor were so garbled that Lori finally gave up, deciding they could manage without him.

She then alerted the passengers to the medical situation and asked if a doctor or a nurse was on board. There was no response until an elderly gentleman stopped her as she passed by. He patted her arm reassuringly while telling her that everything would be all right.

"Oh! Are you a doctor?" asked Lori.

"No, I'm a minister."

"Well, can you help us out?"

"Oh, no, my dear!"

"Well then pray. For God's sake, pray!"

The passenger was moaning in pain when Lori returned to the crew compartment.

"Now, Lori!" said Alyce, who had a weak stomach, "I'm the senior stewardess, right?"

"Right."

"Well, then, you take care of the bottom half and I'll take care of the top half."

"But that's not fair!"

"Everything will be okay! I'll just go get a compress for her head, and then I'll hold her hand."

The plane had just begun its approach to the Honolulu airport when a healthy boy was born. Lori slapped him on the back until he gave his first cry, then tied the umbilical cord with a piece of yarn taken from the argyle socks she'd been knitting and then wrapped him in a blanket.

The passengers had been exceedingly patient despite the fact that they had not been served anything to eat or drink by the preoccupied stewardesses. Everyone was so delighted by the birth that a collection was taken for mother and baby after landing at Honolulu. Captain Lawton supplied the hat.

Transocean People

Edith Nelson, 1946. EN

Refugee Flight, Germany, circa 1948. HGE

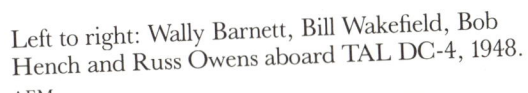

Captain Harvey Rogers, TAL chief pilot. (_____?) in flight uniform. RGM

Left to right: Wally Barnett, Bill Wakefield, Bob Hench and Russ Owens aboard TAL DC-4, 1948. AEM

Captain Dan McCarthy. TNN

TAL Captain Ran Raid and Miss Hawaii. RL

Left to right: Art Ryan, J.W. McCoy and Ted Vinson on a DC-4 somewhere in flight, 1947. RL

"Hopalong Wei," Free China's entry in the International Frog Jumping Olympics at Angles Camp, California, escorted by Elain Tu (Civil Air Transport) and Sandy Weins (Transocean Air Lines). The traveling case in which Hopalong and his understudies were housed during the TAL "Royal Pacifican" flight from Okinawa to Oakland, California, was modeled after the famous Tu Lo Temple of Hopei Province, China, built in 984 A.D. Following the jump for the World Title, Hopalong and Miss Tu put in a series of Hollywood and New York television appearances. AH

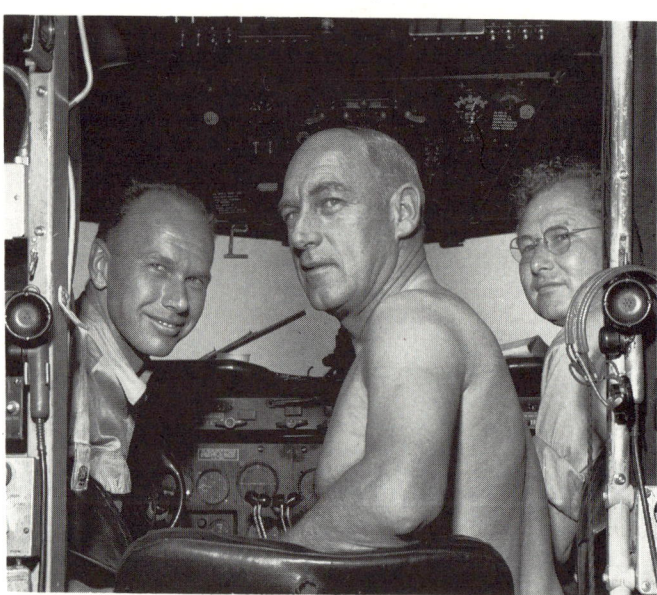

TAL stewardesses Alyce Tokunaga and Elaine Yuen. HGE

TAL stewardesses Pat Lauderdale and Sherry Waterman. Trim uniforms and white gloves were derigueur for TAL stewardesses in the 1950s. RL

Double-Crew Captains Herb Hudson and Joe Stachon preflighting TAL DC-6B, "Royal Hawaiian." RL

Vivian Sims, 1953. RL

Honolulu-Oakland in 6 hours and 53 minutes, a record in 1953. Crew of TAL's DC-6B, left to right: Bill Word, Chuck Smith, Bob Frank, "Dutch" Hasskamp, Howard Moffett and Val Sandidge. RL

Left to right: TAL Radio Operator/Navigator Chuck Sumski, TAL Stewardess Vi Corrington, Captain T.A. Buckelew, Captain Darrell Root. RGM

Left to right: flight engineers Ed Robeson, Fred Fox and Luis Finlason. RL

"Miss Oakland," (Oakland, California), TAL Stewardess Lorraine Mikosch. BA

Flight engineer Bent Elliott.

Four-hour delay, Honolulu. RL

Left to right: Earl De Moe, Carolyn Frisbie, Bob Edgerly, unidentified, Sherry Waterman and Hank Dodson. NE

Left to right: Walt O'Brien, unidentified, John Searles and John Russell. RL

TAL Stratocruiser flight crew, left to right: Bill Piles, John Russell, Burt Elliott and Don Fraim. RL

Waiting for takeoff, Wally Chapin, Bob Glattly, unidentified and unidentified. HGE

-43-

TAL's DC-6B Royal Hawaiian, 1953. Left to right: unidentified, Stan Kochenderfer, Doug Cole, Brenda Reilly, Carol Johnson, Jim Henderson, John Hoenninger, Len Nowell, Bob Judd. Aircraft purchased from Slick Airways for $1,200,000.

Interior of TAL DC-4. HGE

Lockheed 18-40 "Lodestar," 1952, Oakland, California. WTL

TAL C-46F at Oakland, California, 1954. WTL

TAL C-46 N68968, Note the U.S. Flag on the rear fuselage, 1953. WTL

Two TAL DC-4s at Oakland International Airport, May 1955. Color design had changed to red and yellow.
RL

TAL 1049-H Constellation in flight. RL

Chapter Four: Magic Carpet to Mecca
Anything, Anywhere, Anytime

At the Ready

"We'll fly anything, anywhere, anytime." This was the motto of the charismatic Nelson and the men and women who flew to the ends of the earth in the service of Transocean. Their expertise in the mass movement of people, freight, and live cargo was developed by creative planning and by trial and error. But it was the successful completion of the first contracts that established the airline's reputation as "can do" people.

One of the most publicized of the unusual payloads flown by Transocean was forty-five tons of gold bars from Japan to safe deposits in New York. The cache was part of the war booty the Japanese had taken from Thailand and hidden in privately owned vaults throughout Japan.

After the gold was found by U.S. military forces and its ownership established, the Thai government ordered that the treasure be moved to the United States so as to stabilize Thailand's currency on the international money markets. The Federal Reserve System chartered Transocean for the job.

The gold was moved quickly and quietly. Transocean crews flying seven DC-4s accomplished the job in only nine days, each aircraft carrying approximately $6.2 million worth of gold—when gold was $35 an ounce.

Five of the DC-4 transports arrived in Oakland on a Saturday. Because the bullion could not be delivered to New York until Monday morning, Nelson turned the company hangar into a kind of Fort Knox. The police and sheriff's departments were alerted, and TAL guards were placed around the hangar until departure time.

Another unusual cargo was the three planeloads of 100,000 newly hatched chicks. They were destined for the Philippines to replace the poultry stock in that war-ravaged country. The cargo of chicks was so well prepared by Mother Nature that there was less loss of chicks on the flights than if they'd remained in their hatchery at Petaluma, California.

Chicks require neither food nor drink for forty-eight hours after they hatch. This fact of nature reduced the problems of flying them a third of the way around the globe. By the end of their first forty-eight hours after leaving the shell, the chicks had been put in cartons, trucked the fifty miles to the Oakland Airport, and flown 8,800 miles to Manila.

On the return trip to the United States that completed the chick mission, Transocean carried back 774 Rhesus monkeys for use in medical experiments.

Operation Gold Rush—loading gold bullion for shipment by TAL from Osaka, Japan to U.S. RL

These monkeys were used in the development of the Salk Polio Vaccine. They were tarsiers, the smallest of all primates and indigenous to the Philippines. They are nocturnal, goggle-eyed tree-climbers, and they smell. Their odor so overpowered the plane's ventilation system that the crew had to burn their clothes at the end of each leg of the flight. TAL flew in thousands of monkeys from India, Malaysia, and the Philippines for the polio vaccine project.

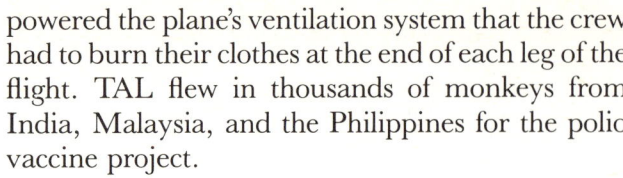

Orvis Nelson congratulates TAL flight crew members Burr Hall, Beau Guinther and Tommy Sconce on safe flight of gold bullion. HGE

Guarding the gold—Frank Soares and Burr Hall. HGE

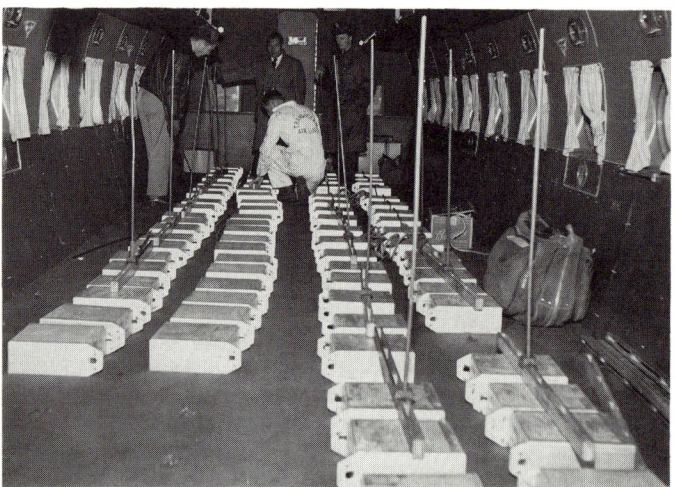

$6.2 million in gold bullion aboard a TAL DC-4, Captain Claude Turner, center. RL

-48-

Crates of monkeys being loaded into TAL DC-4 for flight from India to U.S. for medical research to develop the Salk Polio Vaccine. RL

Monkey handlers wearing gloves and rubber boots look as if they need clothespins for their noses, too. RL

Transocean's "Noah's Ark"

Transocean Air Lines' "Noah's Ark," a DC-4 especially equipped for live freight, made history in 1954. On its first assignment, the big plane "magic carpeted" 550 rabbits, thirty goats, and two million bees from California to Pusan, South Korea, for the Church World Service's Heifer Project, which was established to aid the rehabilitation of the war-ravaged countries of the free world.

The goats traveled in double-deck, pullman style pens designed by Transocean's chief engineer, Al Macedo. The rabbits were placed in lightweight crates and the bees in apartment-type hives fitted with automatic syrup feeders. It was the first mass movement of such a variety of animals and insects, all of which appeared to enjoy the 8,000-mile flight and offered no complaints about the airline food. The goats and rabbits were needed to restock South Korea's livestock. And without the bees to polinate the crops, a food crisis would have made this country suffer even more. Because the bee feeders wouldn't operate at the usual flight altitude, the long flight was made at 4,000 feet above the water.

The operation attracted world wide attention to Transocean. It was covered by all of the wire services, major San Francisco Bay Area newspapers, radio and television stations, and newsreels. One newsreel alone carried it to an audience of 80 million people.

On the return flight, 1,900 monkeys were transported from Manila to Savannah, Georgia, for the National Foundation for Infantile Paralysis' Polio Serum Project. In May, Noah's Ark returned to the Pacific to transport another 1,900 monkeys to Savannah for the foundation's research program.

Transocean flight crews made many discoveries about animal and insect life while flying Noah's Ark. These "facts" were reported, tongue in cheek, in the June 1954 edition of the Taloa Newsletter: Monkeys smell worse than goats and should be made to rig up and operate their own ark, if there's another deluge; goats are more prolific than rabbits and led their highly touted and long-eared rivals by three blessed events to zero in the transpacific productivity derby; bees mind their own business, never bothering anyone while traveling.

On another flight carrying things zoological, TAL Flight Operations in Oakland lost track of one of the DC-4 transports en route from Manila to Oakland. On board were dozens of various animals, reptiles, and birds consigned to zoos around the country.

After hours of radio silence from the aircraft and from other airports, Oakland received this cable: DELAYED FOUR HOURS GUAM STOP REPTILES IN EMPENNAGE STOP. This message came after a young airport attendant opened the door to the baggage compartment, only to come face to face with a huge lizard. He was so frightened that he screamed and took off running toward the terminal. The flight crew, now experienced as animal handlers, performed a lizard roundup and returned the wily reptile to its cage. The flight continued.

Ferrying twenty-four live lobsters on "Operation Lobster," was a snap compared to hauling reptiles. The lobsters, destined for dinner tables, were flown by Transocean from Bradley Field, Connecticut, to Oakland, California, in the cabin, along with a few crew members returning to home base. The stewardesses on board rearranged the seaweed every now and then so that the creatures could breathe comfortably.

New Horizons

Transocean made newspaper headlines around the world in the summer of 1947 when it signed a contract called "New Horizons" with the Province of Ontario, Canada, for the movement of 7,000 English, Scottish, and Irish emigrants from London to Canada. This was the largest number of passengers transported en masse since the end of World War II. The reason for the exodus from Europe by these emigrees was that jobs were scarce in Europe. They were skilled workmen in their trades, and as Canada was in need of these skills, the move was hailed by both Canada and the countries of origin of these workers.

The original contract was renegotiated with

"Operation Noah's Ark" — goats for Korea. RL

Trans-Canada Air Lines (TCA) as the prime contractor because of some legal problems over landing rights. TCA continued to operate a portion of the flights with their own airplanes, and seven thousand workers were transported from the U.K. to Canada.

William R. Rivers was assigned to New York to administer the New Horizons contract. Rivers had been designated by Orvis Nelson as the payee for all funds paid by the United Nations Relief and Rehabilitation Administration (UNRRA). Soon after, Nelson left for Spain leaving Rivers to face a most unusual dilemma.

"Since our company had no credit cards to buy aviation fuel from the oil companies at that time, I had extracted an agreement from UNRRA to pay us in cash, as I had to furnish each outward-bound crew with at least $6,000 expense money," said Rivers.

"Nelson had planned on his return to Oakland to have TAL's board of directors authorize me to deposit and withdraw funds on Transocean's behalf. As it was, the money piled up each time a flight was completed, and Nelson was still in Spain. Bankers informed me that if I deposited the money in TAL's name, I wouldn't be able to withdraw any to pay bills. Similarly, if I deposited it under my own name, then happened to be run over by a car, the company couldn't get the money.

"Finally, I bought a cheap briefcase which I hoped would attract only pity from the New Yorkers on the streets. Wherever I went, the money went. Every morning I rode the subway to Lower Broadway, and sometimes that shabby little briefcase contained over eighty thousand dollars. When I'd return to the Century Hotel, just off Times Square where I was staying, I'd toss my briefcase carelessly onto the counter and ask for a safe box. This way, if I lost it, the hotel had it insured.

"When Nelson returned, he traveled with me to the office near Lower Broadway. I said nothing about the money until we were secluded in my office, then I opened this dud of a briefcase and showed him just under fifty thousand dollars from which I'd have to finance two crews that day. His eyes popped out, and he started to give me a tongue lashing until I reminded him that he had caused the problem. I told him that if I hadn't transferred a hundred thousand dollars to Oakland just a few days earlier, I'd have been carrying around a hundred and fifty thousand dollars.

"Nelson left for Oakland that day, and the following day the bank and I received confirmation that I was now a banking agent of Transocean's. With all that money safely in the bank, I went out and got 'pie-eyed.' The end of this episode was the prompt securing of credit cards from three of the world's largest oil companies."

Flight to Freedom

Impressed by Transocean's competence in moving the 7,000 British immigrants from London to Toronto, the International Refugee Organization in Geneva awarded a contract to Transocean in August 1948 for the first large-scale movement of displaced persons from Germany to South America.

The contract called for 25,000 D.P.s to be moved from Munich to Caracas, Venezuela, with flights leaving Munich daily. Feeling locked out of such a large and lucrative contract, steamship lines persuaded the IRO to reduce substantially the number of D.P.s to be carried by air. But despite this reduction, Transocean continued to fly D.P.s to Venezuela and other South American countries, and to the United States, well into 1949.

The D.P.s were not Germans but Poles, Latvians, and Hungarians who had fled to the West in search of freedom. They were a cross-section of the population and had lost all their possessions either to the Germans or the Russians when their homelands were invaded during World War II.

Whenever a country is experiencing political unrest or oppression, there is always an exodus of its educated and its wealthy. On one of the flights to Caracas, Stewardess Meda Soares found five passengers aboard who could speak English, of whom three were doctors.

Meda learned that the first doctor was a neurologist and had studied medicine in Vienna. He had practiced in Latvia for twenty-one years before the war. Next to him was his wife, a general practitioner. Their only treasures of a once prosperous life—other than the memories they held in their hearts—were a silver ring, a crystal glass with Latvian symbols, and a Latvian coin.

Then the woman introduced Meda to her brother. He too was a doctor, a gynecologist. He had been married to a woman whose family spoke publicly against the policies of the Communist Party now ruling Latvia. Eight months after their marriage, his wife and her family were deported to Siberia, and he was never to hear from her again.

"They were such a pathetic looking group of people that you wanted to do as much as you could for them," said Meda. "The majority wore whatever

1948, refuge orphans in Germany ready to board a TAL DC-4 for a new life.
HGE

clothes they could find, and they lacked toilet articles of any kind. Even the babies did not have nursing bottles. I saw many mothers pouring milk from a cup into a nipple for their babies. And one young father was overjoyed to find an empty soft drink bottle at the airport in Gander, Newfoundland. I saw him wash it and fill it with milk for his baby."

The summer of 1948 also witnessed the beginning of Transocean's movement of 600 students to Europe under contract with Youth Argosy, a non-profit organization devoted to arranging summer travel abroad for college students and professors. Planeloads of students toting bicycles and knapsacks were flown from Connecticut to points in Europe and then returned to the United States several months later. This was the first transatlantic aircoach service.

The Hajj Airlift

The first large contract Transocean was awarded in the Middle East was flying the hajj in 1948. The pilgrimage to Mecca that every Moslem is expected to make once in his or her lifetime is known as the hajj. It has been an annual religious rite for more than 1,300 years with some devout pilgrims crossing mountain passes as high as 19,000 feet and crossing hundreds of miles of desert once marked by the footprints of their forefathers.

Cooperating with Iranian Air Lines, Transocean flew a few flights during the hajj season in 1947, but 1948 saw air transportation play a major role in the pilgrimage. The airline used three C-46s and two DC-4s in the ferry operation between Tehran and Jeddah.

Because non-Moslems are not allowed to see or enter Mecca, Transocean planes landed at the Jeddah airport, thirty miles from Mecca. There, busses transported the pilgrims to within ten miles of the holy city. From that point they were required to walk to the Kaaba, the sacred Moslem shrine toward which all Moslems turn when they pray, then continue their hajj to "Arafa," a place on the Hill of Mercy on the road from Mecca to Taif. Every Moslem who is able is bound, once in his life, to fulfill the "stand at Arafa" or to engage a substitute to fulfill it for him.

The pilgrims came aboard the modern DC-4s garbed in flowing robes and carrying prayer rugs, praying stones (replicas of the black stone in the Kaaba in the center of the holy city), small cooking pots and braziers, and black umbrellas to protect themselves from the scorching desert sun. Their ways were strange to the crews. Some of the passengers spat on the seats, floor and walls. They also built camel-dung fires on the cabin floor to cook their meals, which, when discovered, were immediately extinguished by crew members amid much shouting and shaking of fists by the hajiis.

On the return trips, flight crews had to remove forcibly the heavy packages of souvenir sand the pilgrims were attempting to carry home from Mecca. None of the passengers understood English nor were they able to comprehend that the aircraft could not take off with the excessive weight of the sand on board.

But among the aggravations of the heat and

inability to communicate were a few lighter moments. One of these moments occurred when a pilgrim plane landed for the night for refueling in preparation for the next day's flight. The passengers deplaned to kneel in rows on the runway to pray. The navigator noticed that they were not facing east, as was their custom, and tried to point this out to one of the men by gesturing toward the stars. Then organized confusion reigned as one by one they realized their mistake and turned to face the east. They appeared to be saying to one another, "Hey! Turn around—we're facing the wrong way. Pass it on!"

On another trip the pilot had difficulty holding a steady course as from time to time the plane would dip unexpectedly for no apparent reason. Nothing seemed to be wrong mechanically. The crew was puzzled until it was discovered that the reason for the mysterious movement was the Moslems shifting the weight as they knelt to pray. As the devout Moslems did their five daily prayers, the crews learned to expect the aircraft's respectful dip.

Captain Bill Keating was in trouble from the first day he flew the hajj. One of the Transocean airplanes flying the run to Jeddah had lost an engine on takeoff at Teheran and had returned to the airport for repairs. The necessary work could not be accomplished for several hours and so the evening flight to Jeddah was canceled. Meanwhile, a large group of pilgrims with tickets to Jeddah rushed the plane, trying to get on board, and nearly caused a riot when they were denied access. To them, the trip was the dream of their lifetime—and they wanted to depart immediately.

The police were called but were unable to control the crowd. Finally, Keating and TAL's Jack Ullner, who was in Iran handling the accounting for the hajj, boarded the aircraft and let the pilgrims file in until the plane was filled. Then Keating started the engines and taxied to the end of the runway where he conducted preflight procedures, then quickly flicked off the switches on the outboard engines—causing them to backfire and shoot long tongues of flame past the cabin. After he had done this a couple of times he swung the plane around and taxied back to the terminal. This action convinced the pilgrims that the plane couldn't take off. But they refused to disembark, staying on board until the morning departure.

Transocean's participation in the hajj continued for ten years. One year they flew the two thousand members of the royal household of Saudi Arabia's last reigning monarch, colorful King Ibn Saud, from the thousand-room winter palace at Riyadh, the capital city of Saudi Arabia, to his summer palace at Taif. A fleet of twenty airplanes were required to complete the operation by flying a total of sixty flights over a two-day period.

The number of Moslems flown by Transocean and other airlines during the hajj numbered in the hundreds of thousands. Exact figures are not known because of the many different points from which the operation was conducted. But the number of pilgrims visiting Mecca during the hajj of 1948 was said to have exceeded five hundred thousand.

Berlin Airlift

On June 21, 1948, Stalin blockaded Berlin, Germany's former capital and home for 2 million people in its western sectors. Before the blockade, these people had been sustained by three land routes through East Germany to West Germany, but access on these roads had to be granted to each

Hadjiis descending a vertical ladder at Jeddah after a flight via Transocean. They are making their holy pilgrimmage to Mecca, the Holy City, and carry portable cooking braziers, and the ever-present black umbrellas for protection from the intense desert heat. Most of the Hadjiis had never flown in an airplane before, and attempted to build fires on the cabin floor to cook their meals. RL

vehicle and its occupants by the Soviets. Suddenly, Stalin closed these supply lines, expecting to starve West Berlin into submission.

Without food, coal, medical supplies, or clothing, the Berliners and Allies faced two choices: evacuation or slow starvation. As quickly as Stalin had begun the blockade, the U.S. government countered with spirit, zeal, and resourcefulness. By a seemingly impossible feat of organization, an airlift was begun.

Four days after the blockade began, two military C-54s loaded with 20,000 pounds of food and medical supplies flew into Berlin. These were followed by commercial aircraft contracted for the airlift such as seven DC-4s from Transocean. Approximately 8,000 tons were flown into Berlin each day with a landing every three minutes. TAL's aircraft made forty-eight round trips across the Atlantic in 1948 in support of the Berlin Airlift, transporting coal and other supplies.

During the spring of 1949, Nelson again received an urgent message from the IRO. This time they were calling upon Transocean to dispatch twenty-five airplanes immediately to Shanghai to evacuate a colony of White Russians and Jews who lacked citizenship and who were fleeing for their lives before the Communist takeover of Shanghai.

Inflation was rampant in Shanghai at the time, and flight captains carried their expense money around in suitcases. A cup of coffee cost $1 million in Chinese currency. To stop the black market from flourishing, anyone caught dealing in it would be shot by soldiers. Transocean's pilots more than once witnessed executions in the middle of the street.

The operation scheduled four planes out each day and the evacuation to be completed in eight weeks. When the last plane left Shanghai, the Communists were but ten miles from the city.

Transocean Flies the Military.

Several military contracts were awarded to Transocean during its early years. One awarded in December 1948 kept airline personnel working around the clock for days, helping fly more than 30,000 U.S. Army personnel and their dependents across the Atlantic.

There was almost no way for TAL to plan ahead for business. The unexpected job came when Congress voted not to renew the Immigration Act that permitted German girls who marry American soldiers to become eligible automatically to enter the United States. The U.S. Army officers were frantic. They had only a few days to make arrangements to fly thousands of war brides out of Germany before the expiration of the act on Christmas Day.

As Transocean was the only American airline with a station in Munich at the time, it was the first to participate in "Operation Flying Bride." Eventually, eight other airlines participated in this contract.

Mechanics were rushed from Transocean's East Coast division to Germany, and locals were hired to handle the baggage. During that first week, Station Manager Don McAfee was so busy that he didn't have time to take his shoes off. Sleep came in winks on a cot at the office during the entire airlift; while his wife Dorothy took innumerable telephone calls, answered questions and briefed flight flight crews in order to keep the aircraft departing on schedule.

"We were getting a planeload out every hour on the hour, around the clock," said McAffee. "And by the end of it, I was so tired I felt paralyzed."

Korean Airlift

When hostilities broke out in Korea in 1950, records at the Fairfield-Suisun Air Base (now called Travis Air Force Base) in northern California showed that at 6:15 p.m. on June 30, 1950, a TAL Skymaster was the first airplane to take off for Korea and that the second TAL airplane was actually Korea-bound before other carriers had started. That first aircraft carried a cargo shrouded in secrecy: 3.5 inch bazooka rockets. (Some thought Seaboard & Western put the first plane into the sky in the Korean Airlift, but Transocean was first according to Howard Mingos in an article in *Esso Air World*, March/April 1951).

Subsequent TAL planes carried blood plasma, ammunition, and spare engines to the war zone. On their return to the U.S. mainland, they carried wounded personnel and equipment for repairs. This was in support of the Military Air Transport Service (MATS).

During the first twenty-one months of the Korean Conflict, Transocean airplanes carried 7,112 litter patients, 20,000 military passengers, and 9,960,095 pounds of military cargo on 673 flights between Travis Air Force Base and Tokyo. At the height of the conflict, Transocean used seven DC-4s, garnering nearly 14 percent of the airlift activity on the transpacific shuttle.

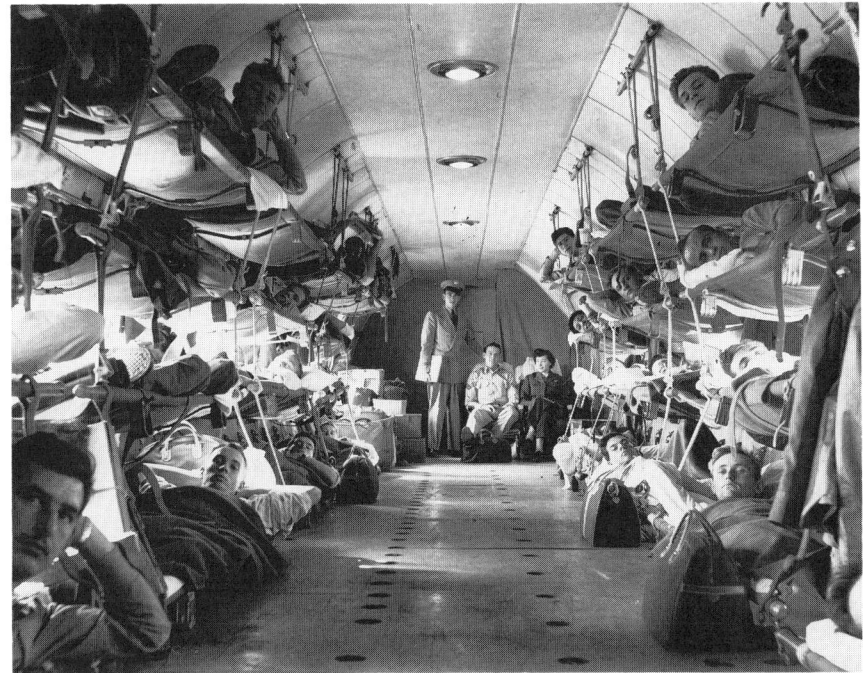

TAL Purser Jerry Orlin with casualties from the Korean Conflict. TAL, under contract with the military, flew hundreds of servicemen back to Travis Air Force Base, Sacramento, California. RL

Diaper Specials

During the late 1940s and early 1950s Transocean's aircraft were chartered by various groups in the U.S. to fly English, French, and German war brides back to Europe to show off the grandchildren. Members of the Britannia Club of Oakland were the first to fly Transocean's "Diaper Specials" in August 1949 from Oakland to London and France via Idlewild International Airport in New York. Of the passengers on board, seventeen were British girls married to American soldiers, and three were French brides. Also along were a number of older women who were World War I brides, twenty-seven children, twelve of them infants in arms, and three uncomfortable men.

Newspaper headlines proclaimed: "War Brides, Tots Fly Abroad—Males Find WAH! Is Hell!" One of the men had accepted a job in England, and one was on his way to propose to his British girlfriend. The third refused to be identified when he climbed into the passenger cabin with the babies, and the myriad cartons of canned milk, emulsified menus, and boxes of cloth diapers on board for the babies' comfort.

Transocean perfected its technique of transporting infants by using DC-4s equipped with "cloud cradles," special bassinets invented and manufactured by TAL which could be suspended in rows from overhead baggage racks.

On the return flight, six weeks later, the *New York Herald Tribune* reported Idlewild in chaos during the nearly six hour lay-over as airsick babies screamed, toddlers fell off counters, and older children clambered through windows when their mothers' attention was diverted to customs and immigration procedure.

Sightseeing for the Sightless

Children were always close to the hearts of the people of Transocean as nearly everyone in the company had young families of their own. Because of the sensitivity and generosity of Nelson and airline employees, eighty-two blind or visually impaired children once realized the dream of a lifetime when Transocean hosted several flights for the children over the San Francisco Bay Area.

None of the children, all between seven and fourteen years of age, had ever been near an airplane before. Nelson and other flight personnel briefed them on all the procedures, from fastening safety belts to preflighting the plane, the engine warm-up, to the let-down for the landing. Even the scenery was described in detail. Before the flights were over, the children could call out changes in direction at the slightest movement of the plane. Back at the gate, each child was taken into the cockpit to sit in the seats and touch the controls.

Not all of Transocean's flying was done for profit.

TAL's "Cloud Cradle" for safety for babies during flights. Testing the cradle is TAL Captain Andrew Madsen's daughter, Lisa, who is with her mother, Marian Madsen. RL

A "Diaper Special" War Bride flight to Europe with plenty of diapers on board. LPS

Pakistani seamen enroute to New York to rendevouz with a freighter. AH

War brides and their children going to see grandma and grandpa in Europe aboard a TAL DC-4. AH

Bill Glenn escorts school children around TAL's hangar area, Oakland, California, 1958. RL

Pat Longhran, Jim Corbett and Gerry Clemente with Bell helicopter for shipment to Japan from Oakland, California, 1953. RL

TAL airlifts electronic equipment for Hawaii's first television station, KONA (now KHON-TV). GEM

Chapter Five:
Wings Over Paradise
The Island Stations

Honolulu, Hawaii

PEOPLE WERE living on the island of Oahu, third largest of the Hawaiian Islands, before 1000 A.D. Called "the gathering place," Oahu lies between Kauai and Molokai. The real meaning of the name Oahu has been obscured from prehistory Hawaii. The sobriquet, "the gathering place," was given to the island sometime in the early 1900s, probably by a Honolulu business man. Honolulu Harbor, discovered just before 1800, became a key Pacific port of call for whalers and sandalwood and fur traders. In later years, Honolulu's John Rodgers Airport became the stopping place for military and commercial aircraft in transit from the mainland to the South Pacific, the Orient, and points beyond. In March 1946, thirteen years before Hawaii became the fiftieth state, Honolulu was not only the first stop on the air route for Transocean Air Lines, but also one of its major bases.

Transocean changed the course of aviation in the Pacific when it created the first ever packaged group tours to the enchanting Hawaiian Islands. These low-cost tour packages enabled vacationers to fly to the island paradise who otherwise might not have been able to afford the trip. The tourist trade, developed out of thin air by the TAL sales department, grew into an important source of revenue for Transocean.

Early in 1953, the TAL sales people organized nine customized Friendship Tours, with direct flights from such out of the way California towns as Fresno, Ukiah, and Chico. The first tour was for members of the Chamber of Commerce of Hayward, California, and departed from the Hayward Airport, the first time such a large aircraft had landed at the small airfield.

Transocean conducted successful tours for several other chambers of commerce in California, aided by a sales blitz conceived by Regional Sales Director Jim Corbett, and implemented by Corbett, Bill Leonard, Ed Hogan, Newell Davis, and the rest of the sales staff. Esther McConnell, who was the company's first tour director, found interesting places in Honolulu for the tourists to visit by enlisting the aid of a Hawaiian taxi driver.

Transocean's luxurious DC-4s and its sleek new DC6B, *The Royal Hawaiian*, carried all kinds of organizations to Hawaii: members of the Grange chapters, The Flying Farmers, football teams, beauty queens, optometrists, Boy Scouts, turkey growers, square dancers, bird watchers, members of The Gentlemen Chefs, the Beverly Hills Health Club, and many others.

Orvis Nelson's ingenuity infected his entire organization. As a result, TAL often made news with "firsts" in the industry. In September 1953, for example, Transocean's low fare of $109 to Honolulu, the lowest air fare to the islands since air service began, made newspaper headlines across the country. Soon after the commencement of the Friendship Tours, Transocean also inaugurated flights between the big island of Hawaii and the mainland, operating one or two trips a month from Hilo direct to the West Coast.

By the end of 1953, industry statistics indicated that Transocean had carried 10 percent of the total passenger business between the mainland and Honolulu that year, a significant statistic for a carrier of TAL's relatively small size when compared to United Air Lines or one of the other scheduled carriers.

The popularity of Transocean's low-cost package tours was proven beyond doubt in 1956 when more than 10,000 passengers traveled via Friendship Tours to Honolulu from March until October.

Max Hodder, of TAL's Los Angeles sales office, followed in the footsteps of Hawaii's early fur traders—only Hodder traded tickets to Hawaii on TAL's airplanes to glamorous movie stars, such as Rhonda Fleming and Linda Darnell, in exchange for the publicity the stars' presence on board would generate for the airline. Additional free TAL tickets were traded by Hodder for office furniture for TAL's Chicago sales office. This trading went on even among the flight crews. For example, it was rumored that a flight crew once traded two bottles of whiskey for an aircraft engine and a new tire out in the South Pacific. The deal included installation.

Honolulu was also the site of an important Transocean maintenance base where repairs and modifications on aircraft in transit and on contract work for the National Guard, the U.S. Coast Guard, and other airlines was accomplished. The first Inspect and Repair As Necessary (IRAN) contract from the Hawaii National Guard was won by Transocean's Honolulu repair station for work on twelve of the Guard's F-86 jet aircraft.

All of Transocean's activities in Hawaii were directed for more than a decade by station managers such as Doug Cole, Pete Rayburn, Gene Cohan, Jimmy Doak, and Dick Laskelle.

Oakland Municipal Airport, International Terminal, tour group flying to Honolulu, Hawaii via TAL, early 1950s. HGE

Inside Oakland Municipal Airport, International Terminal at North Field, tour group waiting to board a TAL DC-4 for Honolulu, Hawaii. Everyone dressed up when flying in the 1950s. AH

Getting the passengers in the mood for a Hawaiian vacation. RL

1953 — Two TAL DC-4s parked at John Rogers Airport, Honolulu, Hawaii. HGE

The Trapp family ("Sound of Music") takes Transocean to Honolulu, Hawaii, 1953. HAP

Canadian Boy Scouts fly Transocean to the Hawaiian Islands. C

Left to right: Andy Cummings, famous Hawaiian entertainer, TAL's Jim Corbett, Miss Hawaii and TAL's Captain Bill Keating. HC

Left to right: TAL's Doug Cole, Esther McConnell and Stan Kochenderfer check out a Hawaiian luau in advance for TAL tour passengers. McC

Members of the Hayward, California Chamber of Commerce make their fourth trip to Honolulu, Hawaii via Transocean Air Lines. HGE

Oakland, California Chamber of Commerce members ready for their second "Friendship" tour to Hawaii. AH

San Leandro, California Chamber of Commerce members arrive in Hawaii, 1958. TNS

Even the out-of-the-way California town of Ukiah took TAL to Hawaii in 1956 where they were welcomed with the traditional Hawaiian lei greeting. TNS

Seattle, Washington, police drill team ready to march up the steps of a TAL Super Constellation to attend the International Police Chiefs' convention in Hawaii. TNS

Lovely movie star Linda Darnell takes to the skies with Transocean Air Lines. Unidentified TAL stewardess welcomes her aboard. RP

TAL DC-4 "Taloa Hawaii" and Pat O-Regan. BC

Beautiful movie star Rhonda Fleming gets a send-off from two of TAL's Los Angeles sales staff, Gerry Orlin and Max Hodder for her trip to Honolulu, Hawaii. SP

One stop shopping in Hilo, Hawaii. One could buy wedding clothes at Anna Mae's, then step next door to pick up a marriage license, plus tickets for a honeymoon on the mainland via Transocean Air Lines. TAL's Doug Cole and Timmie Amai. KB

Wake Island

The first recorded sighting of Wake Island was by the Spanish ships *Los Reyes* and *Todos Santos* in 1568 under the command of Alvaro de Mendana, who named it "San Francisco." Subsequent hydrographic source charts and maps show that it was independently discovered from time to time and named variously Mendana, Lamire (take care), and Discierta (desert), Wake's Wreck, Helsion, Halcyon, and others. It was Captain Samuel Wake who dropped anchor at the island in 1796 in the British trading schooner Prince William Henry. The discovery is now generally attributed to him and officially bears his name.

The V-shaped atoll is the visible top of an inactive submarine volcano whose height above sea level is only twelve feet. Although it is commonly known by one name, it is actually composed of three separate islets, Wake, Peale, and Wilkes. Wake is just four miles long and is a mass of coral rubble, sand, and scaviola bushes surrounding a green lagoon — not much more than a speck at flight altitude.

Wake Island was charted in 1841 by Lieutenant Charles Wilkes during his South Seas exploration when one islet was named for him and the other for Titian Ramsay Peale, the expedition's naturalist. Wake was formally claimed by the U.S. in 1900.

The tiny atoll in the middle of the South Pacific Ocean was home to about 140 Transocean employees during the forties and fifties. There were also several hundred others who worked for Pan American, the Civil Aeronautics Administration, the Navy's Search and Rescue Unit, the Army's Missile Tracking Station, Standard Oil, or other companies concerned with supply, maintenance, or construction on the island.

During Transocean's tenure, Wake was one of the most important airfields in transpacific travel. It's presence was vital in support of the Korean War. Before the advent of jet transports, every flight which crossed the mid-Pacific used Wake as a refueling and/or maintenance stop.

In late 1947, TAL's employees built a complete village on the island. In addition to the usual airport facilities, it included employee housing, a hotel to accommodate 200 guests, a restaurant, and even a small library. The facilities were open to crews and passengers, both military and civilian, who were en

Terminal and operations area, runway in foreground, Wake Island, 1954. RL

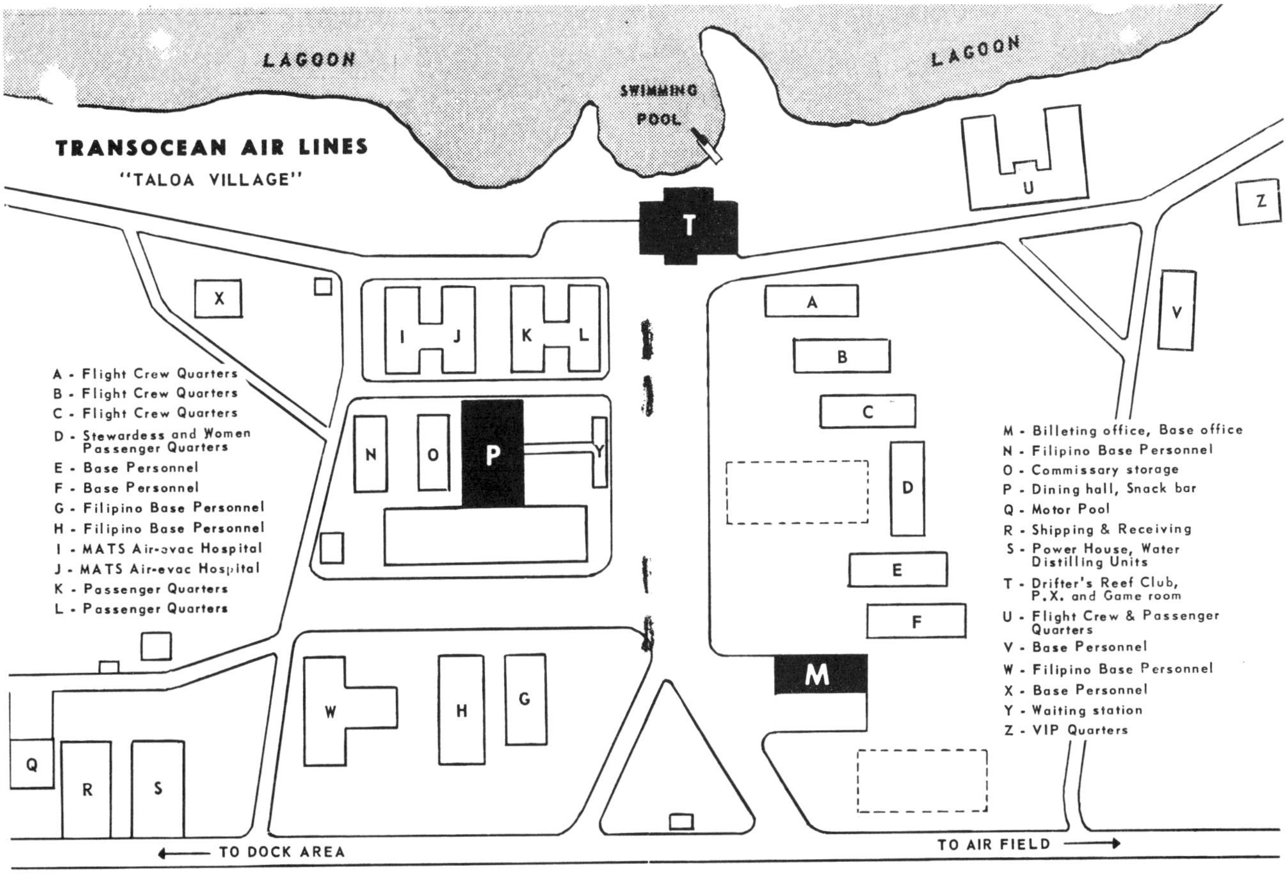
LAGOON
LAGOON
SWIMMING POOL
TRANSOCEAN AIR LINES
"TALOA VILLAGE"
A - Flight Crew Quarters
B - Flight Crew Quarters
C - Flight Crew Quarters
D - Stewardess and Women Passenger Quarters
E - Base Personnel
F - Base Personnel
G - Filipino Base Personnel
H - Filipino Base Personnel
I - MATS Air-evac Hospital
J - MATS Air-evac Hospital
K - Passenger Quarters
L - Passenger Quarters
M - Billeting office, Base office
N - Filipino Base Personnel
O - Commissary storage
P - Dining hall, Snack bar
Q - Motor Pool
R - Shipping & Receiving
S - Power House, Water Distilling Units
T - Drifter's Reef Club, P.X. and Game room
U - Flight Crew & Passenger Quarters
V - Base Personnel
W - Filipino Base Personnel
X - Base Personnel
Y - Waiting station
Z - VIP Quarters
TO DOCK AREA
TO AIR FIELD

Map of Taloa Village, Transocean's compound at Wake Island. HGE

route to other destinations.

Under the direction of Don McAfee, Transocean's Director of Island Stations, and a succession of station managers beginning with Jack Greany, and later, H.G. "Red" Emery, Claude Wall, Larry Bovatt, and "Chic" Collins, the airline provided the high quality service that was expected and even at times when it wasn't expected. They serviced aircraft, loaded and unloaded cargo, and maintained a motor pool of jeeps, trucks, and boomcats. Dispatchers such as Bill Oliver (who had lived on Wake for so many years he was considered the "mayor" of the island), Art Ely, John and Don Willhalm, and Frank Armstrong, were kept busy nearly around the clock. The TAL facility also took in laundry, cooked meals, and its employees were ready to perform a hundred and one other tasks for transiting aircraft and their personnel.

Work at Wake began and ended each day with the station manager making notes on his giant operations bulletin board. It was located in the dining hall, a place where all would pass through several times each day. The bulletin board kept everyone informed of the ever-changing schedule.

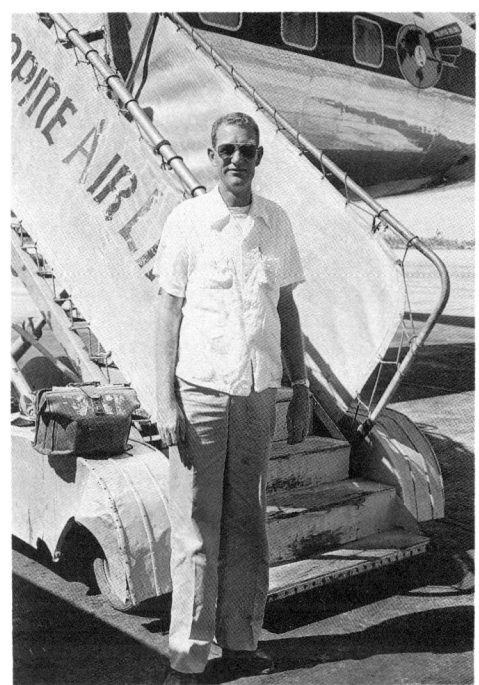

H.G. "Red" Emery, TAL station manager at Wake Island. HGE

By noting the number of departures and arrivals, the port steward could figure how much of the thousands of pounds of food shipped to Wake each month was to be prepared for that day, the number of flight lunches to be prepared for departing planes and when to deliver them to the flight line. The message center also listed for the billeting clerks the rooms in the hotel that needed cleaning because of check-outs. Even the bus drivers knew when to be at the flight line to bring a crew back to the village over the three-mile stretch of dusty road.

Wake Island averaged seventy-five flights each week. Among those seventy-five, Transocean handled its own aircraft, plus those from the U.S. Air Force, Philippine Air Lines, United Air Lines, California Eastern Airways, Seaboard & Western, and Sabena, the Belgian airline.

Once in 1952, the monthly average of about 300 planes increased to 427 due to the Korean airlift. During that four-week period, TAL served more than 30,000 meals, distilled more than 240,000 gallons of water, and housed a daily average of 286 passengers.

Among the many V.I.P.s to visit Transocean facilities at Wake Island were Bob Hope, Jayne Mansfield, Tyrone Power, Linda Christian, U.S. Secretary of State John Foster Dulles, and Eleanor Roosevelt. Major James Devereaux, who was in charge of the U.S. Marines during the battle with the Japanese for possession of Wake during World War II, paid a return visit. President Harry S. Truman and General Douglas MacArthur met there to confer on October 15, 1950. The purpose of the mid-Pacific meeting was for the general to brief President Truman on the chances of the Soviets and Red China entering the Korean Conflict against the United States and South Korea.

Under Wake's usually sunny skies, Transocean promoted the growth of new plants on the island: fig trees, palms, papaya, banyan, and ironwood. The airline's gardener raised radishes, tomatoes, parsley, onions, and other edibles through hydroponics, a method of growing plants in water and nutrients rather than soil.

But on September 16, 1952 a devastating typhoon named "Olive" struck Wake and leveled nearly everything in its path, whether vegetation or buildings. The windmeter at the CAA weather station blew down when the winds reached 163.5 mph before the peak of the storm. They were estimated to have reached 170 mph during the worst of the typhoon.

Mountainous seas and torrential rains battered the island all afternoon along with the howling winds. Most of Wake was still under water seventeen hours after the typhoon struck. People huddled in any shelters they could find. Some managed to make it to dugouts and bunkers deserted by the Japanese in World War II. A number of Transocean's employees headed for the walk-in refrigerators in the mess hall or hid under the heavy tables in the bakery and kitchen. Others built shelters in the warehouse with sacks of sugar and flour.

Houses were ripped apart bit by bit. The island's church sailed out to sea, and the outdoor movie theater was flattened. Trees and bushes were completely stripped of foliage and many were broken; flowers were blown right out of the ground.

Hazel "Mom" Sorensen and her husband Martin, who were in charge of Transocean's commissary and dining room, were among those who waited out the fierce storm in the mess hall. In her eyewitness account of the storm for her hometown newspaper in Minnesota, Hazel wrote, in part:

Movie stars Tyrone Power and Linda Christian riding Transocean's bus, Wake Island. HGE

"Transocean people sat, or rather stood it out just about everywhere they could find a table top or solid thing to lean against or cling to. About half of our personnel found shelter in the refrigerators, which is where Martin and I were. We had to leave the door open to breathe, but when a crash started, we all backed up and closed the door. We were in there from about 10:30 a.m. until 3:00 p.m., and that is a long time to stand up so close together. We stepped out of the refrigerators into twelve inches of water when the storm subsided.

TAL Commissary Dept., Wake Island. Martin and Hazel Sorensen, superintendents, second row, third and fourth from left. Station manager H.G. "Red" Emery, third row, center.

Drifter's Reef, Wake Island. WO

The Windy Palace Movie Theater, Wake Island. HGE

Transocean's dining hall on Wake Island where thousands of passengers were fed. RL

Transocean's little store and lounge, Wake Island, 1948. RL

Transocean's base maintenance personnel, Wake Island. RL

"Later, someone ridiculed the statement that the waves had been twenty feet high, but will someone please tell me how the old landing barge that stood in front of our house got a half-mile away up on top of a fifteen-foot rise? We found three dead fish under our house, and there were ripples in the sand around the mess hall."

Kiku Hori was one of the Transocean stewardesses asleep in her quarters the morning Olive bore down on the island. She was awakened by the shuddering of the barracks building caused by gale-force winds. Kiku was appalled at what she saw when she ventured a look outside. "The rain lashed crazily in all directions. A quonset hut across the way had been ripped off its foundation, knocked over, and was being tossed about like a monstrous tumbleweed.

"Fearing that our structure might meet the same fate, we stews decided to take our chances and seek refuge in the mess hall, the largest building in our compound, about one hundred yards away. We locked arms firmly, braced ourselves against the wind, and cautiously wended our way through the flying debris to safety — we thought.

"Many other huts were being blown apart and the sheets of corrugated tin were flying projectiles in the wind, making the outdoors a veritable giant slicing machine. It was a miracle that no one was killed.

"Once we made it to the mess hall we were fed a hot breakfast by the valiant kitchen crew, and we then attempted a game of poker to keep our minds off the storm. In bidding our hand, we peeled off soggy cards which had been soaked by the constant spray of rain being forced through the screens.

"Suddenly, I was blinded by a solid wall of water. A huge section of the roof had blown off. I felt someone's hand take mine and lead me to a shelter, one of the four refrigerated storehouses for the food supply. The concrete walls were about a foot thick, and the space in each measured about eight by eight feet square.

"It was standing room only except for myself. Being of the smallest of stature I managed to squat in a crate of green onions like a hen about to hatch her eggs. Fortunately, I had had the foresight to bring along a shower cap. I was directly under a leak in the roof and rhythmic plops of rain water dropped onto my head the entire time I was in the reefer.

"Uppermost in my mind was the fact that the highest point above sea level on Wake was twelve feet, and that the slightest tidal wave could swallow the atoll and all of us into the briny blue sea forever.

"As soon as it was safe, ground crews from the compound on the other end of the island, where non-transient personnel were assigned, acted as a rescue squad searching for survivors. They collected the women and children first and took them to their own quarters which had been spared by Olive.

"Some of them came for us to take us to the other side of the island. The ride in the jeep those few miles was like reviewing the aftermath of a blitzkrieg. Hardly a structure stood intact. It was incredible that hardly ten hours had elapsed since being rudely awakened that morning."

Early the next day, Air-Sea Rescue planes from Honolulu's Hickam Field and Kwajalein arrived with food, water, and medical supplies for those marooned on the coral speck in the middle of the Pacific Ocean. That was the first day of a long reconstruction program that Transocean undertook to build a bigger and better Wake Island base.

By 1957, the Transocean facility had been rebuilt and expanded to house 903 persons. Nearly 180,000 billets were furnished that year to transit crews, passengers, and base personnel. The dining room seated 340 people, and Transocean's staff served 812,579 meals during the same twelve month period. Each day, Transocean produced

TAL Stewardess Dee Wheeler and Edward Yamuguchi unload entree for Wake Island Christmas barbecue, 1952. BT

President Harry S. Truman's presidential plane, "The Independence," at Wake Island for President Truman's meeting with General Douglas MacArthur, October 15, 1950. (Note: TAL furnished the President and General with a 1948 Chevrolet sedan to use for holding their private talk). HGE

General Douglas MacArthur, Wake Island, October 15, 1950. HGE

25,000 gallons of water with five 75-kilowatt generators operating at once, and Transocean's laundry handled linen service for the hotel and the personal laundry of 345 employees. The maintenance facility serviced and maintained a total of 6,433 transit aircraft in 1957.

Transocean's Drifter's Reef cocktail lounge, which was also known as "Drifter's Grief" by some, was the preferred watering hole in the South Pacific. It was the proud possessor of a vintage 1896 piano with a history of being dragged back and forth many times between the various agencies on the island.

In addition to swimming, fishing, and collecting seashells and Japanese fishermen's glass floats for recreation, Wake also boasted a motorcycle club, a flying club, and a golf course which was alternately said to have either two holes or nine holes (six when the tide was high), depending upon who was describing it, and named either the Low Tide Country Club or the Hol-Hi Golf Club. But some enterprising entrepreneur decided to have the last word and had caps and membership cards made up bearing the "Hol-Hi" logo. There was also on Wake Island the popular Windy Palace outdoor movie theater, where even the short-legged island dogs sat on the benches to watch the show. And a privately operated radio station, WAKE, played recorded music day and night. Left unattended much of the time, occasionally a tape would stick or break leaving listeners with twenty or thirty minutes of silence until fixed by the engineer.

Practical jokes were a way to alleviate the boredom which eventually plagued those who were on Wake for an extended length of time. One of the most innovative was pulled off by some wag who played a stereo recording of the sounds of trains at a railroad switch yard late one night, much to the consternation of those sleeping in nearby barracks.

Various off-beat clubs were also thought of, to pass the time, although most never materialized. One was "The United Hairless Club of America," to be touted as the first of its kind ever to be organized in the world, and whose object would be to impress the public that club members considered themselves fortunate to be hairless.

The stewardesses' quarters on Wake, where Kiku and the other Transocean flight attendants were sleeping when Typhoon Olive ravaged the island, was known as The Iron Girdle because of its fortress-like appearance. The wood and screen barracks building was entirely enclosed by a fence originally made of the perforated steel strips used for laying temporary aircraft runways during the war and later replaced by a wall of aluminum slats. There was a six foot Cyclone fence surrounding it and a gate topped by a large sign which said: Off Limits To All Males. Powerful spotlights shone down upon The Iron Girdle during the night.

These drastic protection measures were necessary to discourage unwelcome male visitors since there were several hundred men living on the isolated island and very few single women. Before the installation of The Girdle, an occasional male, usually inebriated, would venture into the quarters after dark to steal a piece of highly prized feminine underclothing.

Sherry Waterman Parker, in her book about her experiences as a stewardess, *From Another Island*, recounts the difficulty a more respectable man had when he tried to contact a girl who was inside The Girdle. "He had no choice but to stand outside the outer fence yelling her name, or if he wished to be less conspicuous, try to guess where her room was located and call more softly from that area. Thus, we could hardly consider it uncomplimentary when the young man who was taking us out to dinner would say, 'I'll come by about six and rattle your cage!' "

Aftermath of Typhoon Olive, Wake Island. HGE

TAL's Line Maintenance Hangar, Wake Island. HGE

Bound in opposite directions, two TAL airplanes meet at Wake Island. RL

Guam and The Trust Territory

The Chamorros were the first inhabitants of Guam, and they are thought to have come from Asia in makeshift boats about 2000 B.C. The Portuguese explorer, Ferdinand Magellan, led the first expedition to Guam, arriving in 1521. Spain made the island a possession in 1561 and ceded it to the United States in 1898 after the Spanish-American War. Because of its remoteness and distance from the mainland, it was placed under the administration of the U.S. Navy.

Guam was attacked by Japan on December 7, 1941, and captured on December 10. U.S. forces landed on Guam on July 21, 1944 but did not complete the recapture of the island until August 15, 1944. Guam was a familiar stop for ATC pilots such as Orvis Nelson from the time the U.S. had regained possession of Guam until the fighting stopped the following August.

Operating twin-engine amphibian planes, Transocean's air and ground personnel flew a challenging mission for the United Nations and the Department of Interior after the war by providing scheduled air service to the far-flung Marshall, Marianas, and Caroline Islands of the South Pacific. These islands, which became known collectively as Micronesia, were scattered over 3,000,000 square miles of the Pacific Ocean, but the islands themselves covered just 687 square miles of land area. There were 2,148 islands, atolls, and islets, eighty-four of them inhabited by 51,764 people of mainly Melanesian, and partly Polynesian ancestry.

Orvis Nelson tapped twenty-five year old Captain Edward Landwehr in 1949 for the job of setting up the new inter-island airline nicknamed "The Jungle Airline." He was chosen for the task because of his Navy training and because he had experience flying amphibians. After months of planning, obtaining aircraft, and finding housing for the crews, Landwehr pronounced the airline operational. Within six weeks every flight was filled.

Natives living on some of the more remote islands had not seen an airplane in years, so the arrival of a Transocean flying boat was a social event, with as many as fifty natives paddling their outrigger canoes through the surf or across a lagoon to greet the ship with the same welcome given the trading vessels of the past.

Transocean's planes carried four-man crews and flew a scheduled route transporting ten passengers at a time, along with cargo and the mail.

From their base in Agana, Guam, the flight crews piloted PBYs and Albatrosses on scheduled five-day runs, leaving every Monday for ports of call at Truk, Ponape, and to Majuro, the end of the line some 1,800 miles away. At each island they would remain overnight.

Water landings were made at Ponape, while air strips were used on Truk and Majuro. Return flights were made on Fridays. Scheduled flights

TAL's Terminal at Guam, TAL DC-4 on tarmac, 1948. RL

TAL crew station wagon, Guam. Left to right: John Searles, Frank Ambler and Art Ryan. PR

TAL's Guam Motors, Agana, Guam. BS

Director of Island Stations Don McAfee, center middle row, holds a conference at Guam with TAL employees. FK

were also made to Saipan, Yap, Koror, and occasionally a few of the smaller islands.

Transocean was respected for its on-time schedules, under the direction of station managers such as Jesse Morrison, George Winter, and Dick Laskelle, as well as for the fine aircraft maintenance provided by mechanics Gordon Lincheid, Paul McDougal, Carl Barefield, Gene Weaver, and others. Barefield and Weaver were commended by Trust Territory officials for heroic service beyond the call of duty when they dived under water in a shark infested area to repair the landing gear of one of the flying boats.

The incident occurred when Captain Gil Thomas radioed that his inbound flight from Yap to Guam was having nose gear trouble and would have to make a landing in Apra Harbor instead of the Naval Air Station.

The two men raced to the harbor, stopping only long enough to buy swim trunks and rent skin diving suits and equipment. They were alongside the plane as soon as it skimmed to a stop in the water. One stood guard against sharks and barracuda while the other worked under water on the landing gear. Repairs were completed in forty-five minutes, and the flight proceeded to the air station, arriving less than one hour late.

Mercy flights were undertaken in emergencies to such outermost islands as Tinian, Rota, Ulithi, Anguar, Peleliu, Kwajalein and Ebeye to transport ill or injured natives to a hospital. Transocean once flew milk to the babies of Koror when supplies ran short; another time, they carried medicine to subdue an epidemic of an upper respiratory ailment among the natives on the island of Ulithi.

When a typhoon made the seas too rough for fishing and destroyed the crops planted by the natives of the tiny island of Kili, about 100 miles south of Majuro, a ship tried unsuccessfully for five days to put food ashore before Transocean was called upon. Captain Don Kosteff and his crew fed the people of Kili by rigging a dump chute in the tail of a PBY-5A and jettisoning more than 1,700 pounds of food to the beach through the tunnel hatch.

Leprosy was prevalent at the time among the natives on some of the Trust Territory islands, and a leprosarium at Tinian had been set up for their care. TAL transported afflicted natives there for treatment. Often, the authorities had to search for them for they would hide in the bush because they believed that they would have to stay in the hospital for years away from their families. Their confidence was restored once they were made to understand that the disease often could be arrested and that they could fly back home again if the treatment was effective.

This South Pacific paradise was sometimes marred by crime. At times, Transocean became involved. Once two crew members from a Pacific Micronesian Lines' ship had a fight, and one knifed the other to death. Transocean was called upon to return the body to Manila after first transporting it to Guam for embalming.

Another call to Transocean came when a mentally deranged young man of twenty on Ulithi, found a gun and killed two people, one of whom was a member of the constabulary.

The boy had very long hair and wore only a loin cloth when he was captured. When TAL's PBY crew arrived he was tied to a tree and jabbering incoherently. Then he was led by the police to the flying boat, legs hobbled with a rope and his wrists handcuffed to his guard. The Transocean crew flew him to Guam where he remained under observation in a hospital for several weeks. When his doctors finally decided that the case was hopeless, they recommended that he be returned by TAL to Yap until the mental hospital at Saipan was completed and he could be committed.

Grateful natives often showed their appreciation of Transocean's services by giving feasts in honor of the crews with such exotic dishes as tiny fried bananas, French fried breadfruit, lobster, tropical fruits, and fresh coconut milk to drink.

One native of Angar, an island in the Ponape group, showed his appreciation in a most unusual way. He led a Transocean flight crew to an armed 500-pound bomb, a war remnant hidden in the jungle just a few feet from where Transocean's planes parked for the night.

Lonely families employed by the Trust Territory government on the outlying islands also were recipients of the kindness of Transocean. In December of each year, flight crews would chip in to buy Christmas presents and fly Santa Claus to deliver them to the children of each of the six district centers.

Something unusual happened at the loading dock area of Truk Lagoon one day while Transocean's dispatcher, Stu Jones, was on the island. A large crowd of locals, government officials, kids, and dogs were gathered around a group of natives who had just arrived by outrigger canoe. Jones asked the government man what was going on, and was told that the well-built and tall (for that region) natives had come all the way from Kapingamar-

Captain Clark Dixon and friends, Ulithi, Caroline Islands, 1953. CG

Ray T. Elsmore and TAL Trust Territory contract manager Mal Freeburg negotiated the renewal of TAL's contract with the Department of the Interior. WPS

angi (Kah-peengah-mar-angee) atoll—about 200 miles—for the sole purpose of buying a few cartons of cigarettes. They apparently gave the journey about as much thought as anyone stateside would give to jumping into the family car for a trip to the corner store.

As the men moved about the dock area, the Trukese would part ranks and fall back as if in deference to their stature and powerful physiques. To Jones, the men from Kapingamarangi looked mean and tough.

The Trust Territory official asked one of the men about the object that was stuck in the waistband of his lava-lava (wrap-around skirt). The native produced what he called Kapingi, brass knucks, a deadly device made of a certain tree bark, wrapped in strands of wire and fibers and imbedded with a murderous row of sharks teeth in just the right place.

When asked why they carried such weapons, the native answered, "Because we are such peaceful people." This seemed puzzling to the government man, and he asked what seemed to him a logical question, "Why, then, if you're so peaceful, do you carry such terrible weapons?" The native patiently replied, "That's what makes us so peaceful!"

When one of the aging PBY-5As Transocean had leased from the Navy began showing its age after flying thousands of miles in the service of the natives of the Pacific islands, the aircraft was sold by the Navy as surplus to the Thorne Engineering Company of Los Angeles, California.

The amphibian was being ferried from Guam to Los Angeles by Captain Clark Dixon, copilot Chris Angelos, navigator Bob Edgerly, and engineer Russell Varner when one of its two engines conked out just after it passed the point of no return on the Honolulu-Oakland leg of the trip.

Dixon radioed Oakland that he had insufficient fuel to reach the mainland. A U.S. Coast Guard flying boat was dispatched and soon met the PBY and shepherded it to the freighter *Harry Culbreath Victory* en route from Pusan, Korea, to the Gulf of Mexico. The veteran flying boat put down safely alongside the freighter, despite nine-foot swells, and the crew stepped one by one into the ship's power launch without even getting their feet wet.

The freighter's crew then swung the crippled PBY onto its deck with a crane and continued its journey to the mainland. Cynically, the freighter company later claimed salvage rights and was said to have instituted a lawsuit against the U.S. government.

Crew of this TAL PBY-5A, "Taloa Majuro." Left to right: Norm Ricciardelli, Bob Weidmayer, John Blanchard and Bill Molesworth, Guam, 1952. RL

By June 1954, the first of three Grumman Albatrosses to be certificated by the Civil Aeronautics Administration for commercial operation arrived from the United States to replace the slower PBYs on TAL's Trust Territory routes. The 250-mph twin-engined amphibian had a gross weight of 34,000 pounds, a wingspan of 80 feet, and a range of 2,700 miles. It had gained fame as a military utility transport and air-sea rescue craft in the service of MATS. Later, it had received its certification and modification at TAL's subsidiary, Aircraft Engineering & Maintenance Company.

That same year, Transocean received CAB authority to operate ten round-trip vacation flights between Guam and Tokyo to provide the military and civilian population much-needed recreation and diversion.

Following Orvis Nelson's creed to do honest business anywhere in the world, and to fill a need, aviation related or not, Transocean established a division of Taloa Motors at Agana, Guam, for the sale and service of Dodge automobiles. The Taloa Motors Division newspaper advertisements claimed to "accept anything, absolutely anything, as a trade-in!" Business was brisk.

By the late 1950s, the Trust Territory Division was operating four SA-16 Albatrosses throughout the Pacific. At the end of the decade, when Transocean Air Lines ceased operations because of bankruptcy, the Trust Territory Department of Interior gave TAL employees at Guam permission to continue their services for ninety days until the new contractor, Pan American Airways, could take over. A steering committee for their own management was formed by those TAL employees still at Guam. One of the names for the new TAL operation, submitted with tongue in cheek, was "Tropical Island Transport Service." Trust Territory officials promptly denied the request.

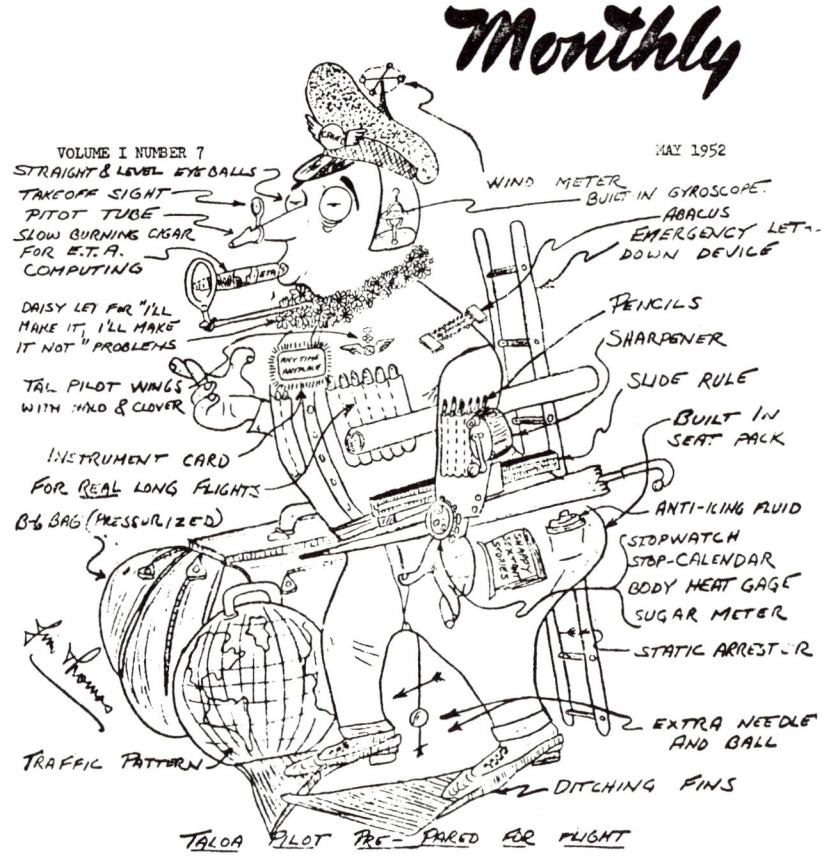

Cover from the *Micronesian Monthly* newsletter, artist, Jim Thomas, 1952. TNM

"Taloa-Ponape," TAL's PBY-5A, flight crew and maintenance people at Guam, TAL's Trust Territory Operation for the United Nations and the U.S. Department of the Interior. AH

These were two of the four SA-16s stationed in Trust Territory.

TAL's Grumman N-9944F Albatross at Oakland, California, 1954. WTL

TAL SA-16 N-9943F at Oakland, California, 1954. WTL

Taloa Motors' at Okinawa, TAL's Jim Kelly, right.
HGF.

Okinawa

Okinawa, an island 370 miles south of Japan, is 65 miles long and comprises inhospitable reefs of coral and rugged, rocky mountain peaks thrusting up from the depths of the sea. It was the site of the bloody World War II battle that began on April 1, 1945 and came to an end late in June. The Japanese fought on land, sea, and in the air literally in a suicidal frenzy. When it ended, about eight weeks after it began, the United States and its allies had suffered nearly 50,000 casualties, and the Japanese had lost 100,000 killed and 7,800 captured.

Just five years later, the reconstruction from the war on the Ryukyus Islands was well under way. Jim Kelly of Transocean's Taloa Motors Division, recognizing the growing need for automobiles, opened an auto dealership on Okinawa, the largest in the Ryukyus chain.

Taloa Motors was the first private enterprise on Okinawa to be issued a business license. The U.S. military, still an occupation force on the islands, and the U.S. Civil Administration of the Ryukyus then gave Taloa Motors permission to import and sell cars with the proviso (under law) that Taloa Motors would import the cars, then sell them to Ryukyu Taxi Company, who would then resell them to the public. Business flourished. Within two years, Taloa Motors had outgrown its facilities and in 1953 began construction of a new building for the dealership in Naha, Okinawa, and new headquarters for the Guam Motors Division in Agana, Guam. This was probably the only time when Americans were successful in exporting cars to the Orient, in this case Dodges and DeSotos.

Tahiti and Beyond

"I thought I was transported into the Garden of Eden," wrote French Admiral Louis de Bougainville, who claimed Tahiti for Louis XVI in 1768 and negated the discovery by British Captain Samuel Wallis one year before. Captain Cook arrived at Matavai Bay in 1769 exploring and charting most of the Society Islands. He named the group after his employer, the British Royal Society.

A 10,000 mile exploratory flight into the South Pacific far south of the equator and more than 1,400 miles off the established airways was completed early in 1951 by the adventurous Transocean Air Lines. The flight's purpose, one of three under a contract with Tahiti-Hawaii Airways, in cooperation with the United States, French, and British governments, was to determine if it was feasible to establish a commercial air service to Tahiti and other islands in the area. Reliable flight service was needed because transportation to Tahiti was irregularly supplied only about eight times a year by cargo vessels. Furthermore, these ships could accommodate a maximum of only nine passengers per trip.

The first of the DC-4 exploratory flights carried Honolulu civic and aviation leaders. It departed from Canton Island, turned southeasterly to an area into which no commercial airliner had ever flown—the French-owned Society Islands—and landed at Bora Bora on a steel Marsten Mat airstrip built by U.S. military forces during World War II. From there, the passengers were transported by boat to Tahiti. The return flight was made via British Samoa and other islands in the South Pacific.

Transocean also carried the first mail by direct flight between Tahiti and Honolulu under contract with Tahiti-Hawaii Airways. At the time, it was the only air service between those two points.

Soon after the first exploratory flight, Transocean completed another off-airway mission by blazing a commercial air trail between Guam and Nandi, Fiji Islands. The purpose was to bring a group of fifty medical students for the U.S. government (under a contract with the High Commissioner of the Pacific Trust Territory) to the Central Medical School at Suva, Fiji, where they would receive the rest of their training.

Five charter flights were also conducted by Transocean during the summer of 1956, in conjunction with Tahiti-Hawaii Air Cruises, Ltd., from Honolulu to Bora Bora. The intriguing itinerary chosen by Tahiti-Hawaii for these charters was "For Men Only." Bora Bora is considered the most beautiful island in the world by many who have visited it, including James A. Michener who believed the island to be "...a scene of positively dazzling beauty!"

Accommodations at this smallest major island of the Society Group were still so primitive in 1956 that Transocean's flight crews lived in tiny grass shacks surrounded by avocados, bananas, gardenias, and orchids. They had to catch rainwater in two barrels, one for drinking water and the other for bathing and washing clothes. They named one of the grass shacks "The Bora Bora Yacht Club."

The airline that had begun without an airplane or a hangar now had a yacht club without a yacht.

Tahiti-Hawaii Airways' South Pacific Exploratory Tour via Transocean Air Lines. BE

Members of TAL's "Bora Bora Yacht Club." Left to right: mascot, Frank Soares, unidentified CAA Inspector, Pete Rayburn, Burt Elliott and Don Fraim. BE

On the ramp at Pago Pago, Samoa. RL

Chapter Six: Land of the Northern Lights
Alaska/Northwest Division

Seattle, Gateway to Alaska

*I*n 1851, pioneers from Illinois founded a settlement along Puget Sound on Alki Point. They chose this site because of the area's many natural resources, but above all others, plentiful timber and water. The next year, they moved the settlement inland to the shores of Elliott Bay and named their town Seattle for Chief Sealth, a Duwamish Indian who had befriended them. The production and shipping of lumber accounted for much of the city's early economic development. But by World War II, aircraft manufacturing had become Seattle's chief source of income. Four years after the war, Seattle, Washington, became an important link in Transocean's world-wide operation.

Although Transocean had already been flying salmon fishermen from San Francisco and Seattle to Alaska during 1947 and 1948, and also had a contract with the Navy Bureau of Yards and Docks, the airline's Alaska/Northwest Division actually had its beginning in Seattle in 1949. At the time, Transocean had won a contract to carry personnel and materials twice weekly between Seattle and Adak, Alaska, for the Drake-Puget Sound Construction Company.

Ray Statton was in charge of setting up a sales office in downtown Seattle while most of the work centered at Boeing Field. Secretary Marge Spinks, dispatch and traffic assistant Newell Davis, and aircraft mechanics Dick Cornell, Bob Larrabee, and twins Darrel and Dean Bunker rounded out the Seattle crew. Also on the Seattle staff were Marie Lowery, Jean Halsam, George Hart, Bill King, Al Sedar, and Hal Markie. Among the flight crew members flying DC-4s on the contract were Captains Claude Turner and Frank Kennedy, First Officer Russ Steinhauer, Flight Engineer Charles "Chuck" Redmon, and Purser Lucky Ward. There was a lot of variety to the cargo they carried: daffodils, newspapers, livestock, powdered milk, dynamite, eggs, geologists to the oil fields, helicopters. Even Christmas trees were airlifted from Seattle to Fairbanks.

Because the office was not fully staffed when it opened, some of the employees assumed double duties. For example, Flight Engineer Chuck Redmon was also the first maintenance superintendent at Seattle. Redmon was followed by D.L. "Doc" Curtis, and later Dave Clayton. Curtis was the person who took the necessary steps to obtain a CAA certificate for TAL's Seattle aircraft repair station, and his work facilitated the later establishment of the airline's station in Alaska. Curtis was the driving force at the Seattle hangar, and his concern for the airline was such that he once borrowed money from his mother to make the Seattle payroll during Transocean's troubled times. Another ONAT/TAL original, Captain William Word, was later appointed manager of the entire Alaska/Northwest Division.

The Seattle operation held contracts for the maintenance of airplanes for Flying Tigers, Alaska Lines, West Coast, and General Air Lines. Commercial, corporate, and private aircraft were also serviced at Transocean's Seattle hangar (which was large enough to accommodate two Stratocruisers). They even worked on planes owned by Bill Boeing, of Boeing Aircraft Company, and Nick Bez, also of Boeing and the Wyman Lumber Company.

Although the Drake-Puget Sound Construction Company contract was not sufficient to justify an Alaskan division of the airline just yet, it was soon to come. Because of the efforts of the newly formed sales staff Seattle would soon become Transocean's door to Alaska.

Seward's Folly

Alaska's recorded history began in July 1741, when Vitus Bering, a Danish navigator in the service of Russia, sailed east from Siberia and landed on

C.L. "Doc" Curtis, superintendent of maintenance, TAL-Seattle. RD

TAL's hangar at Seattle, Washington. RD

TAL's Alaska Division Piper Super Cub 1179A at Oakland, California, 1954. WIL

Hauling Christmas trees from Seattle, Washington to Fairbanks, Alaska. FC

A New Breed of Sourdoughs

In 1950, Transocean was awarded a contract to provide air support for the oil exploration on the North Slope, an area of approximately 90,000 square miles, for the U.S. Navy Petroleum District No. 4, and known as the PET-4 Project. The operation employed a fleet of fifteen airplanes, including DC-3s, DC-4s, C-46s, a ski-equipped C-47, and several bush planes. The old Pioneer Hotel in Fairbanks, Alaska, which had catered to the Alaskan Sourdoughs during the Gold Rush Days, housed Transocean's office and employees. It was also home base for the twenty-five TAL pilots flying the Alaskan supply run, including Chief Pilot Hank Dodson, Tom Nowling, Ed Heering, Earl Thompson, Shelby Pitts, Jesse Morrison, Harry Clark, Paul Soha, Ed Landwehr, Roy Minson, George Dijeau, E.H. "Jock" Johnson, Maurice Carlson, and Charlie Stoudt.

The Fairbanks office also employed several maintenance personnel, plus Dispatcher Forbes Baker, Comptroller Hugh McKinnon, and Secretary Jennie Levy.

Wherever Transocean people went, they were confronted with unique problems. But those who were stationed in Alaska encountered a myriad of surprises and obstacles seldom found elsewhere. Everything in the land of the Northern Lights revolved around the formidable weather conditions. Temperatures routinely dipped to thirty, forty, even to eighty degrees below zero. Work came to a halt when the temperature went to forty

the southern coast of Alaska near the mouth of the Copper River. Trappers followed, gathering the skins of the sea otter and other fur bearing animals to take to Europe where they would be sewn into coats to ward off the winter's bitter cold.

In 1867, the United States purchased the vast and mostly frozen territory from Russia through negotiations led by Secretary of State William H. Seward. Americans thought Seward was crazy to waste good money on land which they felt would never amount to anything. Alaska became known as Seward's Folly.

There came an influx of fishermen from the United States, Russia, and Japan, and soon fishing canneries were established. With the discovery of gold in the Juneau area in 1880, the rush to Alaska was on. The population continued to grow through the years and in 1959 Alaska became the forty-ninth state. Twelve years earlier, a new influx of fishermen headed to Alaska—this time via Transocean Air Lines—from San Francisco and Seattle to Bristol Bay in the Bering Sea. Bristol Bay, which lies just north of the root of the Aleutian peninsula, is a rich source of salmon. Transocean flew approximately 2,000 of the migrant fishermen to Naknek for the annual salmon runs in 1947 and 1948.

After hours at TAL's Fairbanks, Alaska Office. Left to right: Eddie Bonzo, Mrs. Chuck Redmon, Doris Dooley, Don Carson and Russ Steinhauer. DD

degrees below. Winds of 100 mph carried such force as to tear planes loose from their ties. Orvis Nelson claimed to have once witnessed a 145 mile an hour wind roll up a steel landing mat like a sheet of paper—with a two-ton truck inside.

Doris Dooley, who was Transocean's office manager at Fairbanks, had to run so many errands for the airline during inclement weather (often working twenty-four hours at a time) that she routinely kept a jug of isopropyl alcohol at her feet in the company vehicle for use in keeping the windshield clear. Doris had previously worked for Golden North Airlines and when Transocean bought out Golden North in 1951, she somehow became part of the package along with the two C-46s and the office equipment. Doris "clucked-clucked" over everyone in the TAL operation and soon became known as Dooley, the den mother. One person who elicited much maternal attention from Dooley was Bill Drum, who wore so many clothes that he became a cause for concern. She feared that if he ever fell down in the snow, he wouldn't be able to get up.

Bill Drum served for one year as director of operations for TAL's Northern Division. During that time he lived on the top floor of the four-level Pioneer Hotel. "I called the place Downhill Manor," said Drum. "The foundation had tilted so that the floor sloped uphill between the kitchen and the living room, and downhill from the living room to the bedroom. Everybody said I planned it that way!" Drum, who was also executive assistant to Orvis Nelson, was transferred at the end of his first year in Alaska to another division of the airline. Two weeks after he left Fairbanks, the Pioneer Hotel burned to the ground. "Had I been there, I wouldn't have been able to get out," he said. "The windows were taped shut in the winter, and the walls of the building were at least a foot thick and insulated with sawdust, so the fire spread quickly." Doris Dooley had borrowed the office typewriter that night and taken it home. It was the only piece of Transocean's equipment that was left after the fire.

Workers could only stay outside for fifteen minutes each hour, such was the severity of the weather, especially at Pt. Barrow, the northernmost outpost. However, the Eskimo men that worked for Transocean could withstand thirty minutes at the usual twenty-five to forty degrees below zero temperatures.

The flat terrain at Pt. Barrow was frozen during the winter months and enveloped in almost total darkness. During the summer months the ground would defrost revealing spongy muskeg. And the sun would shine twenty-four hours a day.

Ken Armstrong was the first station manager at Pt. Barrow. Most of the maintenance on the bush aircraft there was performed in a hangar furnished by the U.S. Navy. Fred Whitmeyer was the maintenance supervisor, succeeded by Art Leen. Some of the PET-4 planes were ferried south to Transocean's Seattle shops for major overhaul work. Among those other TAL aircraft mechanics of the Northwest Division were twins Darrel and Dean Bunker, Bob Larrabee, Smokey Strobridge, Lee DeMent, and Waly Skudlas. At the Umiat outpost, on the North Slope about 150 miles southeast of Barrow, there were two mechanics and one Eskimo employee.

Bill Drum, director of TAL's Northern Division, 1952. DD

Newell Davis, TAL's Northwest Division, 1951. ND

The Alaska Division

TAL flight crew, Alaska, left to right: Ed Landwehr, Roy Minson and George Dijeau. RL

"Taloa Wake Island" cools off in Alaska. HGE

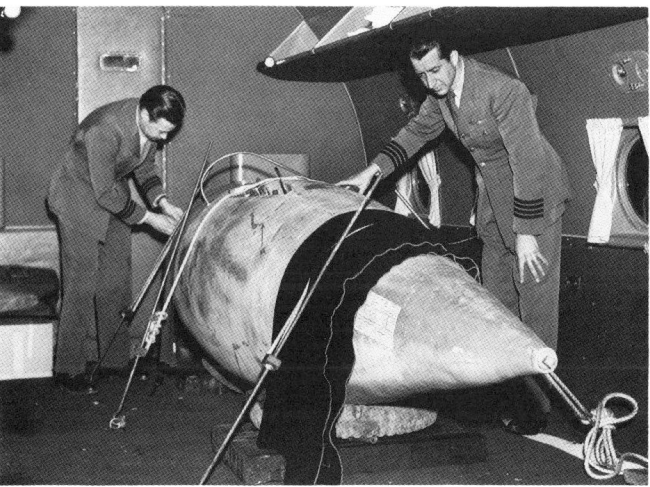

Stalled for two days by high winds on Adak, captains Bob Bunbury and Joe Stachon demonstrated TAL resourcefulness by finding a surplus gas tank at an old Air Force Dump in Alaska. The tank was tied down in the cabin, vented, and connected to the fuel system so the aircraft could continue its flight to Tokyo. RL

TAL DC-3 with skis, Alaska. ND

Helicopter being sent to Alaska for three months of mapping geological sites, 1952. YDR

Rogues of the Red Room

Because the freezing temperatures limited work-time, Transocean personnel had plenty of time on their hands and no place to go. One of the most popular pastimes was playing poker, followed by movies, reading, and occasional horseplay

Newell Davis was transferred from the Seattle office to Pt. Barrow to become the new station manager during TAL's second year into the PET-4 Project. Davis was nicknamed "Mighty Mouse" by bush pilot "Red" Dodge after his temper got the better of him late one December night in 1950, when the horseplay at Barrow got out of hand. Several of the Pt. Barrow men were in the middle of a game of poker in the living room of the pilots' quonset hut. They called it The Red Room, after Dodge painted the walls a bright red. Two inebriated men staggered into the room and fired off a couple of .45 caliber rounds through the ceiling. Playing cards and poker chips flew into the air and onto the floor as the players dove for cover beneath the table. The sound of the shots brought Davis from his room on the run. After persuading the men to sit down and join the game, Davis again left the room for his quarters.

He was almost asleep when the two rogues sneaked into his room and "ventilated" the ceiling above his head. First startled, then enraged, Davis jumped out of bed and without thinking grabbed the .45 revolver, yanked out the magazine, and ordered the men out into the snow without parkas or boots.

Twenty-four hours later, Davis received a phone call from his brother who lived in Anchorage, a thousand miles away. Word had already reached him that Davis had been "run out of the Alaskan territory at gun point." Rumors spread by the Mukluk Telegraph (the airline grapevine), obviously were not always accurate—although Davis's brother did ask to speak to Mighty Mouse.

The Pet-4 Supply Runs

Transocean's pilots flew the PET-4 supply runs between Fairbanks and Pt. Barrow and also between Barrow and Umiat, as well as to many of the smaller outposts. As many as sixteen flights a day were logged as the aircraft serviced these points by landing on frozen lakes after a tractor-dozer (an all-terrain vehicle with tracks, often called a Sno Cat), had cleared a landing strip. For the larger planes this required a 4,000-foot-long swath through the snow and ice depth measured to make sure it was thick enough to hold a 24-ton aircraft.

The Transocean C-47 with skis was based at Pt. Barrow and Umiat. The terrain around Umiat was uneven, but there was a small hill above one of the oil camps. It had a 30-degree slope, and was utilized to ease the job of discharging drums of heating oil. Bill Drum said that the aircraft with skis would land on top of the hill. Then the crew would build a ramp at the door of the plane, tie mattresses to it and roll the oil drums down the hill to the camp.

A number of rescue missions, under the direction of Captain Eddie Bonzo, were conducted using this aircraft. One of the most dramatic occurred when TAL pilot F.E. "Casey" Stengl discovered the wreckage of a Wien Alaska Airlines Cessna 170 while heading back to Pt. Barrow during snow squalls. After radioing the information to Barrow CAA, he continued to TAL's base at Pt. Barrow to pick up Bill English, a Wien Alaska captain, who

A frosty day at Point Barrow Airport, Pt. Barrow, Alaska, 1952. DD

TAL C-46, Pt. Barrow, Alaska. Note original TALOA paint design. DD

TAL at an oil camp in Alaska. Note the oil oozing out of the ground where the flag is staked. ND

Eddie Bonzo and Norm Carmichael, Alaska Division. DD

C-46 N51854, Pt. Barrow, Alaska. Lost RH engine power on takeoff. ND

Nosed over in the soft snow, C-46 N51854 at Umiat, Alaska. CLC

had indicated by radio that he wanted Stengl to fly him to the scene of the crash to see if there were any survivors. Once there, they found the bodies of the pilot and a woman passenger. Just as they turned to leave, English heard the faint cry of a baby. They found the unharmed infant inside the back of the dead woman's parka. English held it in his arms on the return flight to Pt. Barrow. Efforts were immediately begun to locate its relatives.

No radar, ground control approach systems, or other electronic navigation aids existed north of the towering Brooks Range, the last terrain barier en route to Pt. Barrow. The pilots relied on their radio which often faded out, skipped, or played other tricks, and rendered the only two homing beacons virtually useless. They depended primarily upon their own experience and on makeshift signposts. For example, they were the first to discover that every one of the scores of large lakes north of the Brooks Range has a straight side which points directly to Pt. Barrow. The information was of great value to the 3,500 people living in the region.

Every airplane in Transocean's Alaska operation carried a survival kit with rations, candles, heating pots, and snowshoes to keep the pilot and passengers alive in an emergency, and occasionally had to be used. However, there was only one fatal crash during TAL's tenure in Alaska. That occurred when a C-46 transport crashed on December 30, 1952 on top of Chena Dome, a 4,440 foot peak 35 miles northeast of Fairbanks, killing all four of the men on board. The plane was being ferried from Umiat to Fairbanks by Transocean Captain Bob Warren and Copilot Dick Erwin with passengers Dick Cross and Joe Wheeler of Wien Alaska Airlines.

The Intrepid Bush Pilots

The bush equipment consisted of four Noorduyn Norseman, one Grumman Widgeon, one Stinson Reliant, two Super Cubs, and one Travel Air, some of which were leased. Except for the Widgeon, all the others were convertible from wheels to floats to skis, as the season dictated. The skis would more often than not be frozen in the ice whenever the aircraft were preflighted. To release them, the pilots would have to rock the controls fore and aft and spin the prop at full throttle. If that failed, the last man aboard was asked to brave the icy blast and give the tail a hefty sidewise heave. Once the skis broke loose, the aircraft had to be kept in motion or the skis would freeze again—making it tough for the tail-pusher to get back on board.

Bush pilots such as Casey Stengl, Irv Crain, Dan Ackerson, Cyril Seeds, and Red Dodge faced the possibility of forced landings on every flight as they took supplies to the Eskimo villages, or dropped red guide flags ahead of the Sno Cat trains that transported heavy construction equipment and material to the outlying oil camps. The flags marked the course for the 100-ton trains and had to be spotted with 100 percent accuracy, or an entire train might have been sent plunging through the ice into the lakes that dotted the barren landscape.

The procedure whenever one of the pilots found himself facing impossible weather conditions was to radio Pt. Barrow, then pick out what he hoped to be a level spot on the vast snow plain and land to wait for better flying conditions. If the visibility was zero, the pilot said a short prayer and landed anyway.

During one summer a pilot cracked up a Norseman on the Colville River, which flows from the Brooks Range to the Arctic Ocean about 150 miles east of Pt. Barrow. It hit a shallow sand bar, snagged one float, and then nosed over and broke off the float. The engine mount buckled, the prop was bent, and the left wing tip was also torn off. As it was summer and the ground was soft, the rescue squad pulled the wrecked plane up on the river bank and left it there. When the colder weather came, the plane froze into position and the fierce winds of winter could not move it.

TAL later flew several of its Eskimo mechanics to the wrecked aircraft and left them there for a week to repair the damage. Transocean provided them with a portable radio to contact the base and report which parts and supplies were needed as they went along. One of the pilots would fly over the camp in the C-46 every other day to drop food to

TAL bush pilot Cyril Seeds, Nome, Alaska. DD

the men who were working in weather 72 degrees below zero. Once during the work they enjoyed a warm spell when the temperature got up to 55 below. They camped out on the river bank next to the plane, using a tent banked with snow. Stove oil heaters kept the tent warm. The mechanics removed the Norseman's floats, put on skis, installed a new propeller, and patched the broken wing tip.

When the Eskimos had finished their job, Bill Word flew to the site with a new battery. Following normal procedures in the ultra-cold conditions, Word and the Eskimos first checked the spark plugs, heated the engine with a canvas hood and a fire pot, and poured in some hot oil before trying to restart the Norseman's engine. But the battery Word had brought with him was dead. Word tried heating the battery with a blowtorch, without success. Finally, in desperation, he stuck the old battery back. It turned right over, even though it had been dormant for six cold months. Word got the Norseman off the river ice and came zooming over Pt. Barrow, did a chandelle (an acrobatic maneuver consisting of a vertical turn) in celebration and landed on a lake adjacent to the runway.

On another occasion, Red Dodge was forced down by a wall of ice fog some miles out of Barrow in 1952. This incident was typical of what the bush pilots in Alaska faced every day. Dodge made a blind landing, keeping his machine level by instruments and slowing it as much as he could without stalling. He hit the ice hard, bounced into the air and then leveled off for another blind landing. When the airplane came to a stop, the fog was so thick that he didn't bother to get out. He simply sat there until the fog lifted several hours later. Dodge was lucky. The cargo had contained a case of dynamite—and he had literally bounced over a huge crevasse in the ice and landed safely on the other side.

Lady Luck did not always ride with the Transocean pilots of the PET-4 project. When a "nameless pilot" was forced to land in ice fog on the snow-covered tundra about fifty miles from Barrow, he immediately radioed his predicament to the base. He was advised to wait where he was—a rescue team would soon be on its way. But the fog quickly turned into a full-blown Arctic storm, and five days passed before a ground search party, traveling by weasel (Sno Cat) and guided by another aircraft, found the wreck and the pilot.

The only thing that bothered him, said the bush pilot, was his cold feet. He had rearranged the cargo inside the aircraft and climbed into a sleeping bag to read his ever-present Western stories by candlelight. Soon what seemed to be dozens of white foxes took turns coming to the window for a sniff before they circled the airplane and settled down to keep an eye on him.

Though the North is a land known for tall stories, Orvis Nelson swore to this final note in the account of the bush pilot's rescue: When Transocean's chief pilot at Barrow telephoned the pilot's wife to report that her husband had been marooned on the ice for some days, but that rescue operations were under way, the lady reportedly snapped, "That's the first time I've ever known for sure where he was, and that's a damned good place for him"— and hung up. Safely back at Pt. Barrow after the rescue, the bush pilot asked for a new supply of Western paperback books.

Top: Noordyn Norseman N61321, from Alaska Division. Photo taken at Oakland, California. This Norseman plus N49375 and N75938 were later sold to Ontario Central Airlines for $50,000. WTL

Bottom left: Grumman "Widgeon" G-44, Oakland, California, 1952. WTL

Bottom right: De-icing the wings of a Noordyn Norseman with a rope, Alaska. ND

Chapter Seven: TAL—The First Aviation Conglomerate
The Subsidiaries

From Barber Shop to Broom Factory

KNOWN THROUGHOUT the industry as the flying airline president, Nelson was the only top executive of a major airline during the late 1940s to hold transport pilot ratings. The number one globe-trotter spent much time away from his desk in search of business or visiting Transocean's far-flung outposts, all the while keeping an eye out for profitable enterprises to add to his ever expanding international business empire, or airplanes to add to the fleet.

Soon after taking to the skies in 1946 to fly anything, anywhere, anytime, Nelson began to expand into other areas, usually with great success. But by the mid-fifties and after acquiring several subsidiary businesses, some of the men closest to Nelson began to express concern that perhaps Transocean had over-diversified its resources and that the company was in danger of decline. Nevertheless, from its inception in 1946 until as late as 1959, Transocean basked in the glow of spectacular success in most of its endeavors. The airline and its divisions often received commendations from both military and civilian groups for its contributions to aviation.

Hangar 28

Transocean's maintenance and engineering division was established in July 1946 to service TAL's airplanes at Hangar 28 near the company's headquarters in Oakland. The aircraft mechanics built and overhauled engines on top of sand bags until there was enough money to buy engine stands.

The first major conversion project completed by the newly formed maintenance and engineering department was turning a war-surplus B-17G, owned by Colonel Andres Soriano, into a private plane. Transocean's connection with Soriano, the president of Philippine Air Lines, had begun when Transocean helped establish PAL in 1946. Knowing that Soriano's hobby was aerial photography, director of maintenance Al Morjig and his men removed the bomb-bay door from the generously-windowed nose section of the aircraft and transformed it into a luxurious parlor with comfortable chairs where Soriano could take in-flight photographs.

Concerning alterations of a more practical nature for that aging B-17G, chief engineer Al Macedo designed and developed methods whereby a Jack and Heintz hydraulic auto-pilot for automatic flight control could be installed by the aircraft mechanics of Hangar 28. This was a first for such an aircraft.

By the end of 1952, under the guidance of Morjig and Macedo, Transocean's team of precision aircraft mechanics and other craftsmen (such as Bill Glenn, Dave Cook, Dave Tyler, and Mike Lewis), had accomplished many notable feats. One of these was the transformation of a wrecked airplane known as *Kansas City Kitty*. Nelson found the aircraft, a DC-4, in a field while traveling in Kansas, tracked down the owner and purchased it.

Bill Word and a crew were sent to fly it back to Oakland to be rebuilt. What they found was a derelict with broken windows, electrical wiring dangling throughout the cabin, and the landing gear locked in the down position. They managed to fly the wreckage back to Oakland despite these obstacles, arriving nearly frozen and looking distinctly battle-fatigued. Just the ghost of an airplane, it was one of the most unusual looking craft ever to taxi through Transocean's hangar doors. In just six weeks, new engines were installed and all of the repairs made up to airworthiness standards. *Kansas City Kitty*

Colonel Andres Soriano, president of Philippine Air Lines and owner of the San Miguel Brewery, sent his personal plane, B-17G NL68269, to Transocean at Oakland in 1947 for overhaul and refurbishing. WTL

"Kansas City Kitty," a DC-4 put into first-class shape by TAL's Hangar 28 maintenance and engineering team. BE

emerged from the hangar as a first-class airplane and became an important addition to the airline's fleet.

Perhaps the most well known and exotic of Transocean's conversion projects was the *Flying Palace*, the personal aircraft of Saudi Arabia's King Ibn Saud, who, during his reign, unified six million people scattered over 900,000 square miles of desert.

Transocean sold and delivered to the Saudi government, five DC-4s the last of which was the million dollar flying carpet that the 72-year-old monarch would use to travel between his winter palace at Riyadh and his summer palace at Taif, 500 miles away.

Painted on the plane's vertical stabilizer was the gold, white and green royal crest with crossed swords and palm tree. The 50-foot long royal cabin contained a bedroom with a double bed, a swivel throne on a dais (the throne was actually a customized barber's chair) in which the King could turn to face the holy city of Mecca. There were also eighteen foam-cushioned chairs for guests, plus sleeping quarters for a four-man crew.

A folding elevator (copied from President Franklin D. Roosevelt's personal presidential plane, the *Sacred Cow*), was designed by Max Elbaum, chief engineer at TAL's Connecticut division. The elevator was installed at the rear door of the aircraft to allow easy access for the King, who was crippled with arthritis. His first test of the elevator, with his bodyguards and family in attendance, was a tense moment for Sam Wilson as he threw the switch to lift the King. When the mechanism worked smoothly and without a hitch, Wilson breathed a sigh of relief, fearing no longer for his life.

Far-fetched though it may sound, Nelson once bought the fuselage of a DC-4 that was in use as a hot dog stand near Oklahoma City. Those who knew him were not surprised. Nelson scrounged parts and engines to make it flyable. And when it had been reassembled by Transocean's maintenance and engineering team, it went to work flying around the globe as *Oklahoma City* with the rest of TAL's fleet.

Miracles became routine for Transocean's Maintenance and Engineering Department. The

Hangar 28 maintenance and engineering team pose beside King Ibn Saud's Flying Palace. AH

Installing the King's throne, at TAL's Bradley Field, Connecticut maintenance base, 1952. Max Elbaum, center. RL

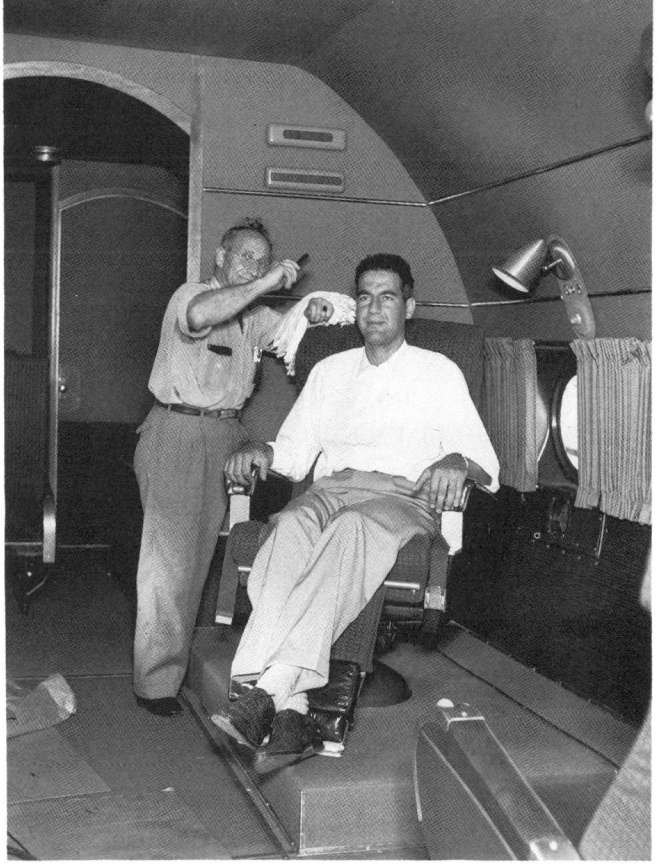

AEMCO's Sam Besser, left, and TAL superintendent of maintenance, Al Morjig, test the barber chair throne before delivery to King Ibn Saud, of Saudia Arabia. RL

King Ibn Saud of Saudi Arabia, the monarch who, during his reign, unified six million people scattered over 900,000 square miles of desert. RL

King Ibn Saud, of Saudi Arabia, tries the elevator on his personal plane. TAL's Sam Wilson is at the controls. RL

rebuilding of a "damaged beyond repair" DC-4, owned by Resort Air Lines, once again proved their remarkable skills. The aircraft was parked at the Municipal Airport at Ogden, Utah, where it had been heavily damaged upon landing. The entire front end, from the bulkhead just behind the cockpit door, was gone, and had to be rebuilt from that point. When TAL's assistant superintendent of maintenance Mike Lewis and the crew of ten mechanics arrived at Ogden that January day in 1953 to dismantle the aircraft for shipment to Oakland, it was parked in two feet of snow. Within ninety days after its arrival at Hangar 28, the aircraft was ready to fly again.

Later that year, Transocean completely built an aircraft from parts scavenged from around the world — it is believed that this was the first time that an airline successfully built up a complete airplane in this way. The project began when one of TAL's executives heard that a fuselage, center wing section, and tail section from a late model Douglas transport were in storage in Argentina. It was owned by Lee Mansdorf and Company, a broker of used aircraft and aircraft parts.

The machine was first owned by the ATC and used in World War II, after which it was declared surplus property and sold to the government of Argentina, which had luxuriously fitted the aircraft to serve as the personal transport of President Perón. It was later sold to Lee Mansdorf and Company. When Transocean purchased it in September of 1953, the disassembled aircraft was put aboard a freighter bound for Oakland, California. Once in Oakland, the three sections were barged up the Oakland Estuary to a point near TAL's headquarters where they were trucked to Hangar 28.

Reminiscent of kids putting a model airplane together from the hundreds of pieces in a box, the men in the maintenance department found themselves faced with the task of cataloging the thousands of parts needed to make this huge transport once again flyable. It was a massive job that called for a lot of attention to detail and much patience. For example, Bill Dell and Bill Baty spent three weeks sitting in the center section of the fuselage just untangling the thousands of cables coiled on the floor like a mass of spaghetti. When the cables were reconnected, every one of them worked flawlessly. In only two months and four days, the Transocean crew had assembled a CAA certified DC-4.

Named the *Argentine Queen*, this reassembled DC-4 was one of Transocean's most dependable aircraft for years. It was later chartered to Airwork Atlantic, Ltd., and with a TAL crew on board for training, inaugurated that company's transatlantic freight service on March 1, 1955. The Argentine Queen was operated by several airlines after TAL's demise and crashed at sea 700 miles west of San Francisco on March 28, 1964.

Transocean Air Lines was known around the world for its innovative approach to accomplish its mission. The story of *Benny Big Feet* illustrates this. *Benny Big Feet* was a C-47 at TAL's Alaskan operation at Pt. Barrow. It was brought to Hangar 28 at Oakland where it was transformed into a ski plane. This would make it possible for the C-47 to land on

Sections of a Resort Airlines DC-4 being transported to TAL's Hangar 28 for repair after an accident at Ogden Airport, Odgen, Utah. RL

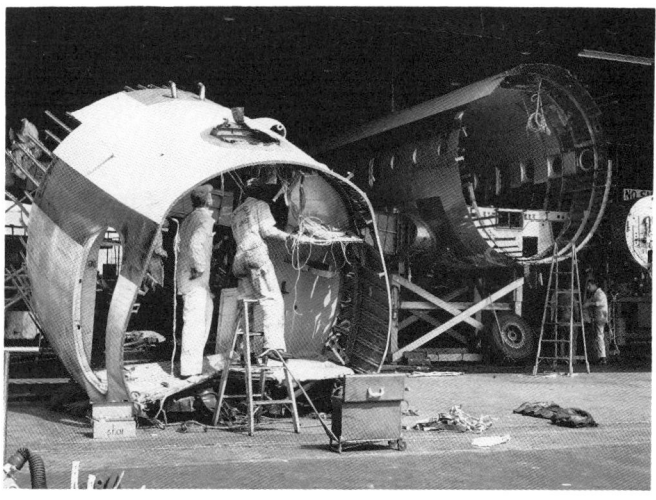
Mechanics at work on Resort Air Lines' DC-4. RL

The "Argentine Queen," a DC-4 being completely rebuilt by TAL at Hangar 28. WD

The "Argentine Queen" comes together, 1953. RL

Rebuilt at Hangar 28 by TAL maintenance and engineering, the "Argentine Queen" is ready for its first flying test. The total job was completed in just over two months. Captain Bill Keating ready to taxi out, 1953. The "Argentine Queen" later was flown in the movie "The High and the Mighty." RL

Fuerza Aerea Argentina DC-3 with skis installed by TAL mechanics at Hangar 28, Oakland Municipal Airport, Oakland, California. AH

the snow on the North Slope. The installation of skis was also repeated by TAL for the Argentine government.

The impossible was always being turned into reality at Transocean. A refueling stop at Keflavik, Iceland, by a TAL DC-4 was the stage for yet another miracle.

When the aircraft was ready to depart after servicing at Keflavik, the pilot misunderstood a signal from a member of the ground crew and taxied straight into a flight line power unit. One of the airplane's wings burst into flames. Fueled by the leaking gasoline, the flames threatened to consume the entire aircraft. However, they were stopped when the damaged wing burned to within one foot of the fuselage.

Al Morjig, from Oakland, was at Keflavik and he wired Orvis Nelson and Al Macedo the details of the accident. Macedo determined that the aircraft could be salvaged by splicing a wing onto the fuselage—until then an unheard-of operation in view of the extensive damage.

Macedo, twenty-three mechanics, and a machinist immediately left for Iceland with the pieces of a salvaged wing. Within hours of their arrival in Keflavik, the mechanics stripped off the burnt wing while Macedo began the engineering work at the navigator's table inside the aircraft. With directions from Macedo, the mechanics began piecing together the wing. When they had built a complete wing it was raised into place and carefully spliced onto the fuselage.

Then there were innumerable delays until approval of the engineering for the four wing splices by Douglas Aircraft Company finally was forthcoming. This approval was necessary before the CAA would issue a certificate of airworthiness for the aircraft. CAA officials might have had their doubts about the safety of the spliced wing but not the test pilot, Macedo, Morjig, and the team. The test flight was an unqualified success, and another footnote was added to Transocean's list of accomplishments.

Madsen Lights and Other TAL Inventions

Another of TAL's accomplishments was an extensive research project in 1955 which resulted in the development of a revolutionary system of aircraft collision avoidance equipment. Although the famed scientist and inventor, Harold Edgerton, had developed the strobe light, Transocean was the first airline to apply this technology.

One of Transocean's flight captains, Andrew Madsen, had thought of the idea for such a system when he viewed a strobe light demonstration in a display window of a photography shop in Frankfurt, Germany, during a layover on a military flight to that city. Upon his return home and over the following months, he began to draw plans for his system and acquired the equipment necessary for his first installation. Madsen's garage was turned into an assembly shop for his project.

Several months later, the first aircraft avoidance system was installed on TAL's 756 by Ray Babb and his crew at Hangar 28. It consisted of seven white strobe lights with a combined candlepower of four million. Each light was placed at a particular point along the top or bottom of the fuselage. Forty times a minute these lights would flash in sequence, one at a time, moving from the

Night test of the Madsen Lights, Oakland, California. RL

Left to right: Al Macedo, Bill Leonard, Al Morjig, Bill Word and three unidentified military men check out the Jato bottles TAL installed on U.S. Navy DC-4. AH

A small bird built her nest in TAL Beechcraft. Maintenance man Bert Homan removed the nest everytime the engine had to be started, then put it back again. RL

Left to right: Luis Finlason, Ralph Padilla, Ray Babb, Al Gnudi, unidentified, Hans Knupfer, Iver Reinika and Barney Neilsen, Hangar 28, 1952. AH

Oakland Aircraft Engine Service cylinder stockroom. RL

TAL radio repair shop, Oakland, California. RL

TAL's Mike Lewis with United Air Lines' representative. TAL held an eighteen month contract with United for the overhaul of their entire DC-3 fleet. RL

tail toward the nose of the plane. This would display the motion, direction, and attitude of the aircraft to any other aircraft within line of sight.

After extensive testing by Transocean, the Civil Air Administration ordered the Madsen Lights, as the system was referred to, so that it could be tested at its center in Indianapolis, Indiana. After an inspection and evaluation was completed in the laboratory, more tests were conducted on a CAA plane under flying conditions. The system was approved and immediately began to attract attention throughout civil and military aviation.

As the news spread throughout the aviation industry, Transocean began receiving orders for the Madsen Light System. United States Steel Corporation was the first to have it installed on one of its corporate aircraft, a Lodestar, and soon the flagships from industry giants such as Signal Oil Company, Morrison-Knudsen, and United Air Lines were seen taxiing up to Hangar 28 for similar installations.

These intensely bright, pulsating lights are now used in other systems in aviation. Frequently they can be seen flashing in sequence as runway approach lights. They have been installed along the Panama Canal to facilitate night passage of ships, and they have even been installed on satellites to flash while they circle the earth.

Another innovation by Transocean's maintenance and engineering division was the development of the first auxiliary ferry-fuel tanks. These tanks could extend the range of an airplane between refueling stops. They could be installed and removed quickly and were primarily used for delivering aircraft across the Pacific Ocean. The first to receive this modification was a Martin 202.

Taloa Academy of Aeronautics

Taloa Academy was the first division created by Transocean. The year was 1946. It was established to provide ground and flight training for the airline's flight and operations personnel. As the school grew, so did its reputation. It achieved acclaim from airlines around the world and from foreign governments for the quality of flight crews it graduated.

Headquartered in a barracks building at the north end of the field at Oakland International, the academy became one of the largest flying schools in America. In 1950, it purchased the assets and name of Moreau Flying Service, one of the oldest commercial flying services on the West Coast, and merged it with its own.

The Taloa Academy established branch offices and training facilities at Minter Field in Bakersfield, California. This school was licensed by the Civil Aeronautics Administration (CAA) to operate with the following ratings: primary flight, commercial flying, and basic and advanced ground school.

The academy was first directed by retired U.S. Air Force Colonel Roger Q. Williams, author of *Half Way to the Moon and Back*, a book written about space travel at least ten years before John Glenn circled the earth. Later Taloa Academy was directed by Herbert Webb. Many of its students were military veterans who qualified under the G.I.

Taloa Academy of Aeronautics, Oakland International Airport, Oakland, California. HGE

Bill of Rights for the government to pay for their schooling. The school offered a wide range of aviation-related courses so that upon graduation, its students would be certified for either flight crews, ground crews, or flight operations.

The first major training contract won by the Taloa Academy was from the government of Indonesia for the training of sixty cadets, who were to serve as the nucleus of that country's newly established military and civilian flight programs. Their training at Minter Field began with "classrooms in the air," sixty hours of flight training in Aeronca aircraft. The second phase of training was conducted in Boeing PT-13D airplanes, powered by Lycoming 225 hp engines. In addition to the flight training, the cadets received ground training in navigation, air regulations, meteorology, and special instruction in American history and English. English is the diplomatic language of the world, but it is also the international aviation language, used by control towers, ground control stations, and aircraft the world over—which explains the English requirement of the academy.

Many of those cadets who were trained at Taloa Academy are now ranking senior officers in the Indonesian Air Force. Several were among the first pilots hired for Indonesia's Garuda Airways, which is still in operation today.

Other contracts from foreign countries included the training of fifteen pilots for Japan Air Lines—all of whom were Japanese air veterans who had been grounded since the end of World War II;

pilots and flight engineers for Lufthansa; and helicopter pilots for South Korea. By the end of its first six years of operation the school had trained more than 1,400 students from ten nations. At its peak, the academy employed more than thirty-five on its staff and had a fleet of fifty-six airplanes.

In 1951 the Taloa Academy began classes for pursers, stewardesses, and flight attendants, under the direction of Gwendolyn Raymond and Kayle Hailey, both registered nurses. The curriculum included aeronautical indoctrination, international documentation, inflight meal service, flight emergency procedures and medical care, inflight service, professional etiquette, appearance, charm, poise, and airline operations.

U.S. Coast Guard personnel on flying status were trained for wet ditching at the Taloa Academy at Oakland. This instruction included taking aloft a crew of four or five pilots to 1,500 or 2,000 feet so that they could observe the pattern of the swells on the surface. The plane would then descend to ten or fifteen feet above the water to show the Coast Guardsmen the flat spots between the ocean swells where they could "dunk" safely in an emergency.

In August 1958, the U.S. Army completed a two-year training program conducted by the Taloa Academy that involved more than 2 million miles of instrument flying. Under contract to the Sixth Army, the academy trained more than 200 commissioned aviators as instrument-rated pilots; they received both flight and ground school instruction from Emmett Fall, Joe Pruszynski and other academy instructors.

Because of the airline's many DC-4 flights over the Pacific route to the Orient, TAL's training division saw the necessity for a flight simulator which would duplicate flight emergencies and procedures while safe on the ground.

Operating under Transocean's "can do" creed, Frank Grinnon saved the company much of the million-dollar purchase price of a flight simulator by building one. Assisted by Burt Elliott and Harry King, it still required 2,500 man-hours and the cost of surplus parts and instruments. Their efforts produced a working mock-up of a DC-4 cockpit with standard layout and instruments.

In addition to training TAL's crews, the academy also provided Link Simulator training for the flight crews of other airlines such as Overseas National Airlines, U.S. Overseas Airways, and California Eastern Airways, as well as private and executive pilots. The simulator was referred to by the pilots as The Monster. A newspaper reporter once said of the machine: ". . . it'll do anything except fly and tell your mother-in-law her age."

Colonel Roger Q. Williams, first director of the Taloa Academy of Aeronautics, and instructor Ed Gribben teach model airplane building to youngsters at the academy facility. RGM

Herbert Webb, director of the Taloa Academy of Aeronautics, Oakland, California. FC

Taloa Academy of Aeronautics takes to the skies above Oakland, California, to advertise its motto. AH

Taloa Academy of Aeronautics instructor Virgil Simmons, right, shows an unidentified U.S. Border Patrol official how to use E6B computer. RL

Emmett Fall instructs Army students at Taloa Academy of Aeronautics. RL

Taloa Academy of Aeronautics instructor Burt Elliott and student in TAL Link trainer. HGE

Graduation ceremony for Indonesian cadets at Taloa Academy of Aeronautics, Minter Field, Bakersfield, California, 1951. HGE

Mary Janislawski instructs students in navigation at Taloa Academy of Aeronautics. RL

U.S. Army graduates of the Taloa Academy of Aeronautics. RL

Robert Lang congratulates Republic of Korea graduates of Taloa Academy of Aeronautics. HGE

Stearman training planes in formation, Taloa Academy of Aeronautics, Minter Field, Bakersfield, California. HGE

TAL dispatcher L.N. Forden with Shirley Williams, Taloa Academy of Aeronautics. LNF

"Coffee, tea or milk?" Stewardesses in training at Taloa Academy of Aeronautics. Instructor Betty Langdale, students Ruth Card, Lorraine Sharp, Salme Tomson, Marcelle Malmendier, Anna Baxter, Anne Keogh, unidentified. RGM

TAL wet ditching drill in San Francisco Bay off South San Francisco shore, 1956. The ditching trainer is an ex-TALOA aircraft, N-93061. It was burned in a hangar fire at Southwest Airways' SFO hangar on Dec. 30, 1955, and the fuselage was turned into that ditching trainer, painted orange, and floated with barrels in the lagoon off the Coast Guard Air Station at SFO.

"Down the chute" training drill, Taloa Academy of Aeronautics. RL

TAL stewardesses participating in wet ditching drill, San Francisco Bay. LP

Atlantic-European Division

Transocean's Atlantic-European Division (AED) was established in 1947. The location of its first headquarters was Teterboro, New Jersey, but was later moved to Bradley Field, Windsor Locks, Connecticut. This move helped to supplement Transocean's West Coast commercial operations and aided in expanding the airline's services to the Atlantic Seaboard and Europe.

By 1953, the highly successful AED operation, which included Flight Enterprises, Inc. and the Transocean Air Lines Overhaul Agency, had 160 employees and had outgrown its facilities. The organization was moved to another compound with hangar and office space that were used by work shifts around the clock, seven days a week. Employment increased from 400 to 4,000 between 1956 and 1958, with a $4 million payroll. By April of 1958, the company had provided millions of passenger miles of transatlantic airlift for MATS under a contract calling for a series of Constellation flights from New York to Frankfurt and Manchester.

The TALOA-Bradley facility was the first aircraft maintenance base in New England to be approved by the CAA for airframe and instrument overhaul. Accessory and radio ratings were later added to expand TAL's services. Among the numerous jobs performed by the Transocean Air Lines Overhaul Agency at Bradley Field was the overhauling of five R5C-1 aircraft (U.S. Navy model designation of a C-46 aircraft), as well as radio transmitters, dynamotors, and oscillators. DC-4 and C-46 aircraft were also serviced by the overhaul agency for the Argentine Aeronautical Commission, as were airplanes owned by U.S. commercial airlines. The AED also operated maintenance repair stations at U.S. Air Force bases in South Carolina and New Jersey to service MATS C-121 aircraft.

In 1949, Superintendent of Maintenance Harry Gorski and his team introduced what was probably the first movie projector and screen on board an airplane. It was installed on a DC-4 owned by the Pakistani national airline during overhaul of the aircraft at TAL's Bradley Field operation. After the first showing of a short movie on the equipment, the PAK-AIR representative turned to TAL's projectionist and asked, "How come you got no Mickey Mouse?"

Under the leadership of President Edward Ringo and Vice President Don Zipfel, Flight Enterprises soon became the largest Air Force contract overhaul firm on the East Coast and one of Transocean's most profitable subsidiaries. Flight Enterprises continued in business well after the airline's demise in early 1960.

Donald C. Zipfel, director of operations, TAL's Atlantic-European Division and Edward W. Ringo, vice president. HGE

Aircraft Engineering & Maintenance Company

Transocean employees at the headquarters in Oakland remember well a certain day in May 1948. Orvis Nelson called a meeting of the 800 employees of the airline and its new subsidiary, Aircraft Engineering and Maintenance Company. His podium was an engine stand in the middle of AEMCO's half-mile-long overhaul line in Hangar 5. The purpose of the meeting was to ask the employees if they would lend to Transocean the money needed to acquire an Air Force contract for AEMCO. The awarding of the contract was predicated upon the company having $75,000 in the bank to provide adequate working capital. But Transocean didn't have the funds, and Nelson had been refused a loan by banks.

With only one day left to win the contract, Nelson made an emotional appeal to the employees in a last-ditch attempt to get financing. He told them that in exchange for their contribution, the company would share half the profit for the first nine months of the Air Force contract.

In an outpouring of confidence, the employees pledged $100,000. On the next day, Orvis Nelson had the required $75,000 in the bank and the contract in his pocket.

The original contract was for 8,000-hour overhauls of forty-five C-54s. It was later revised to require each of those aircraft to be reconditioned every 1,000 hours. Each one passed through AEMCO's 15-station repair system, built around a production

Don Zipfel and Tommy Walker discussing installation of King Ibn Saud's wheelchair on the "Flying Palace." RL

Dispatch office, Bradley Field, Connecticut. Left to right: Tom Sayers, Jack Chack and George Pohle. RL

Unidentified Bradley Field, Connecticut seamstresses. HGE

A hot August day at Bradley Field and time for an ice cream break. RL

During a break period, four of TAL's AED employees look over an article on Transocean in the *Saturday Evening Post*. Left to right: Florence Lynch, Florence Kotowski, Terry Ferrera and Alice Marconi. RL

Ray Del Monte, graveyard guard at Bradley Field, decided that tomatoes might go well for a midnight snack. He wasn't available for the picture, so his fellow guardsman, Julius Berman, day guard, stood in for him. RL

Aircraft Engineering & Maintenance Company, U.S.A.F. T-33s on AEMCO's "moving overhaul line" at Hangar 5, Oakland, California. RL

line concept that had been developed by Chief Engineer Robert Lang and a contingent of AEMCO employees. Headed by maintenance superintendent Ted Borgard and assistant superintendent Ralph Frey, the station repair system won acclaim for excellence within aviation circles because of the man-hours that could be saved using the "moving" overhaul line. A different style of the line was set up for each type of aircraft, DC-4s, F-100s, T-33s, and others. During 1958 and 1959, AEMCO overhauled (under an Inspect and Repair as Necessary contract) 100 T-33 aircraft each month.

Operation Vittles

When the Soviet Union blockaded Berlin on June 25, 1948, AEMCO was awarded a contract for the maintenance of the military airplanes flying the Berlin Airlift to provide life-saving food, medical supplies, and coal to the beleaguered city during the freezing winter of 1948.

One problem the mechanics encountered was coal dust deposited in the interior of the aircraft. One C-54 yielded 243 lbs. of coal dust when it was cleaned. It was packed in jars and given away to employees as prizes in an incentive program. The idea was a hit. The Berlin Airlift contract ultimately enriched AEMCO by nearly $6 million dollars.

The men on the overhaul line became attached to one C-54 they named *Workhorse Harry*, a venerable flying machine which flew the last official airlift flight to Berlin. When it entered the overhaul line the men painted a sign on its nose, "Last Vittles Flight — 1,783,572.7 Tons Airlifted to Berlin." Harry had made 1,943 flights. In the month of February 1949 alone, it completed 194 flights from Frankfurt to Berlin during the massive effort to bring relief to the West Berliners.

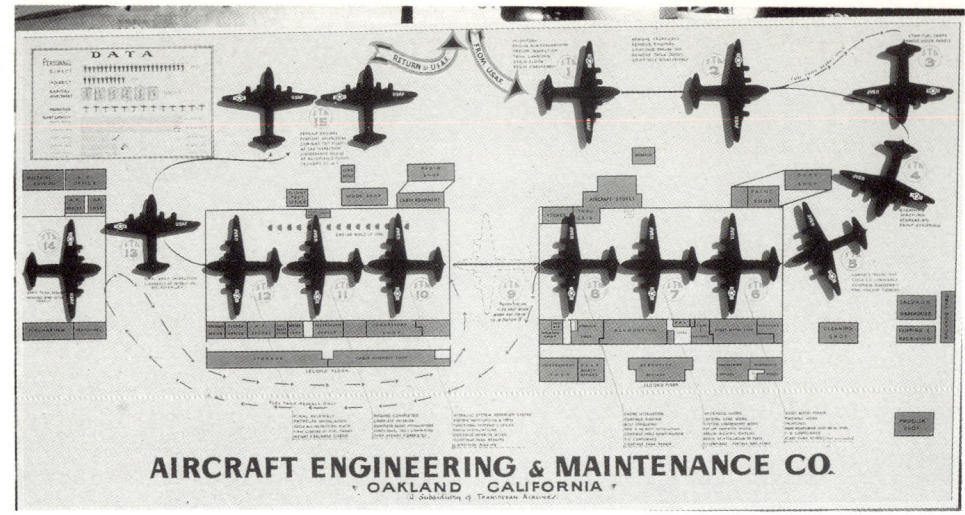

Diagram of one of AEMCO's moving overhaul lines. HGE

Making plans for AEMCO, left to right: Sherwood Nichols, Orvis Nelson, Ray T. Elsmore and Ted Borgard. RGM

A.G. Cole, president of AEMCO. AH

AEMCO's assistant superintendent of maintenance, Ralph Frey. HGE

Orvilla Swiger and Sam Besser, Trim and Upholstery Shop, Oakland, California. RL

AEMCO's Allan Barrie, second from left, and Douglass Johnson, right, note arrival of first C-82 at AEMCO under contract with USAF. RL

AEMCO's welding shop. KRP

AEMCO mechanics, Hangar 5, Oakland, California. AH

The propeller shop at AEMCO. RL

AEMCO seamstresses. RL

AEMCO employees, left to right, bottom: Nettles, Wackrow, Foster, Tompson and Wai. Top: Yee, Adams, Gracy, Krug, Hawkens, Ferriera, Bock, Himenes, Stoner, Wilson, Caires and Lewis. AH

USAF Douglas C-74 undergoing overhaul at AEMCO. HGE

Along the AEMCO overhaul line. RGM

Sherwood Nichols, center, by "Workhorse Harry," last aircraft to fly the Berlin Airlift. RGM

Another internationally known division of AEMCO was Skyscape Interiors by AEMCO (Trim and Upholstery Division), which was founded and headed by Will Aaseth. Known for its luxurious interior decorating of executive and military aircraft, Skyscape Interiors refurbished President Eisenhower's aircraft, the *Columbine*. The aircraft was formerly President Franklin Roosevelt's *Sacred Cow* and featured a built-in bed behind a painting on the wall. Every aircraft redecorated by the Trim and Upholstery Division of AEMCO was designed with soothing colors and custom-built interiors that included upholstered divans that could be converted to berths; retracting polished wood tables; a stainless steel buffet and refrigerator; draperies, and radio and television consoles.

Many time- and money-saving devices and manufacturing techniques were developed by Superintendent Sam Besser and his crew. One of these ingenious ideas, the "hidem" solution was used to secure fabric to the insides of airplanes being plushed instead of the old-style trim tracks. With approval by the Army of the "hidem" technique, Besser was able to eliminate the installation of thousands of screws. He also invented the small press which allowed one man to use the new technique, instead of two or three as previously required.

AEMCO's Trim and Upholstery Division also manufactured the "Child Eze" chair, designed by Howard Mackey and advertised as a Christmas gift for youngsters.

Sam Besser was a quiet but effective boss who instilled a family feeling among the craftsmen who decorated airplane interiors. One seamstress even thought the Trim and Upholstery Division was the finest department at AEMCO. "It's got them all beat for friendly relationships," she said. "They'll have to burn the joint down to get rid of me!"

In 1952 the renowned Stanford Research Institute of Menlo Park, California, contracted with AEMCO for all ground and flight operations connected with their "flying laboratory," a C-54 aircraft on loan to SRI from the Air Force for electronic research. Most of the projects were classified information. On the flights of the C-54 flying laboratory, many advanced electronic devices were tested.

AEMCO was also awarded a $3 million dollar contract to recondition sixty-eight U.S. Air Force twin-tailed C-82 Fairchild Packet Transport planes. These troop and cargo carriers were frequently referred to as Flying Boxcars because of their 2,916 cubic feet of cargo capacity. Military freight could be loaded into the Packet through two clamshell doors which opened up the entire rear of the long, square-side cargo hold. Self-propelled vehicles such as jeeps, trucks, and bulldozers could drive in under their own power. The C-82 could carry forty-two paratroopers with full equipment. It could also tow two Army gliders with personnel and equipment. Rigged as an ambulance plane, the C-82 could accommodate thirty-four litter patients and four attendants. Specially-designed strap suspension litters could be installed in twenty minutes.

Because of the growth of AEMCO during the fifties, it had outgrown its facilities at the Oakland International Airport. Recognizing AEMCO's needs, in 1958 the Port of Oakland built one of the world's largest hangars at a cost of over $1 million dollars. Designed to accommodate the largest airplanes in service and those still on the drawing boards, the hangar measured 225 by 260 feet. Its roof was supported by the largest cantilever span of any building in the United States and allowed complete entry for aircraft with wingspans of 160 feet. The doorway was 50 feet high and 200 feet wide. In addition to the new super-hangar, the port leased an additional twenty acres to Transocean.

AEMCO's first project in the super hangar was a contract with MATS for the modification and technical order changes on C-124 Douglas Globemasters. These aircraft were designed to carry more than 200 troops or 50,000 pounds of cargo at over 300 mph. They had a wingspan of 174 feet and a gross weight of 180,000 pounds.

Other AEMCO contracts included: PARC (Periodic Aircraft Reconditioning Cycle) on Convair C-131 hospital aircraft, the first to be awarded to a civilian contractor for progressive maintenance on this type; rehabilitation of Lockheed F-80 jet fighters under a contract from the Mutual Defense Aid nations; and the processing of 3,036 Air Force T-33 jet trainers under a four-year contract that contributed more than $32,000,000 to the economy of the San Francisco-Oakland Bay Area.

"Child-Eze" chair, designed by Howard Mackey and manufactured by AEMCO's Trim and Upholstery Shop. It was advertised as a Christmas gift for youngsters. Orvis and Edith Nelson's daughter, Holly, seated in one of the chairs. EN

During the early 1960s (after AEMCO had been taken over by the Atlas Corporation), AEMCO assumed management of the U.S. Air Force aircraft maintenance facility at Chateauroux, France, under a subcontract with the pioneer French manufacturing firm of Louis Breguet. Douglass Johnson and Stan Morketter headed up the operation. The Aircraft Engineering and Maintenance Company (AEMCO) continued in business, rather like a postscript to an historic enterprise, until 1964.

Oakland Aircraft Engine Service

Incorporated in January 1949, OAES handled maintenance and overhaul on military and commercial aircraft engines. William R. Rivers, one of the TAL originals, was named president of OAES after the reorganization of the company in 1952. Under Rivers' leadership, the company made

Aerial photograph of Oakland Aircraft Engine Service facility, Hegenberger Road, Oakland, California. RL

many contributions to aviation maintenance. One of the most notable was the development of a self-propelled, mobile aircraft engine test stand that saved over 3,800 man hours per year. Its design greatly reduced the noise produced by aircraft engines at airports equipped with engine repair facilities.

These units were assembled on cut-down, surplus military busses and were equipped with quick-change fittings and the latest instruments for checking engine performance. They carried their own fuel load and could be driven on the highway for work at any point accessible by ordinary vehicles. A complete engine change could be made in just forty-five minutes using these customized units, and their mobility made it possible for the engines to face into the wind at all times, an advantage for accurate testing.

Possibly the most novel of OAES's money-making projects was "Operation Used Wind," brainchild of Bill Rivers. An engineer from the Dinwiddie Construction Company called on Rivers to request help in testing the side panels and windows that were being designed and manufactured for the new Equitable Building in San Francisco. The construction company needed data on how the windows could withstand severe wind and rain storms. The engineer explained that he had stood behind one of the small private aircraft as it taxied away from him at the airport and found that the it had generated enough wind pressure to enable him to determine the degree of water and wind-proofing needed. Now he wanted Rivers to assist him in obtaining one of the small planes and tow it to Emeryville (near Oakland) to participate in the test.

Rivers had a better idea. He drove the engineer to a spot near the OAES testing area where Fred Quinn was installing onto the test stand an R-2800-B series engine from a Flying Tigers transport. They stopped about forty yards behind the testcell. From there they could feel the force of the wind, yet were far enough away to not be struck by the blowing oil.

When Quinn wound up the engine, the blast of wind battered the engineer and sent his hat flying. This only caused him to become more and more enthusiastic. So when Rivers suggested that

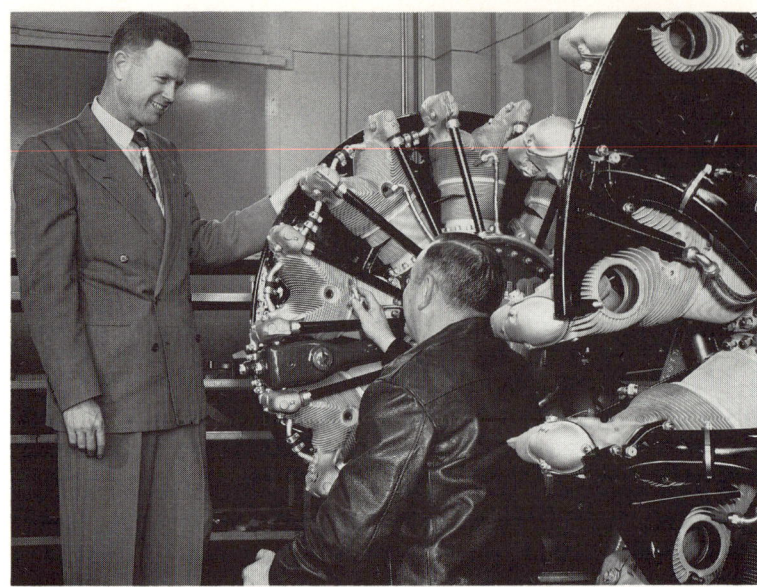

W.R. Rivers, president of Oakland Aircraft Engine Service and Howard Shelton. RL

Oakland Aircraft Engine Service facility. RL

OAES engine test stands. RL

OAES stockroom. RL

OAES could request a highway patrol escort and drive the testing truck directly to the test site, the engineer quickly agreed.

Later, with the windows and the aircraft engine in place on the mobile unit, the test windows were blasted with 100 mile an hour winds. Water was injected into the wind stream to simulate rain. Operation Used Wind netted a sizeable fee for OAES.

In 1958, OAES provided direct support to America's efforts to put manned vehicles into outer space. This support took the form of experimental plating with gold, silver, rhodium, and other metals to learn their relative ability to resist heat.

In addition to its large engine overhaul and research activities, OAES also manufactured and distributed General Electric reciprocating engine aircraft ignition systems and parts under a ten-year exclusive contract with G.E.

There were other Nelson-inspired enterprises too numerous to describe at length. **Transocean Engineering Company** (TEC), founded in 1948 and directed by Harold Hudson, engaged in general construction and the installation of air navigation and lighting systems. TEC completed various bridges in California, including one across Butte Creek, and the Big Bar Bridge in Shasta-Trinity National Forest. In 1954, TEC built roads at Redding, California and Middletown, California, and a $275,000 fish hatchery. But perhaps TEC's most outstanding success was the 6,400 square foot quonset hotel built in just twenty-two days at Wake Island.

The TALOA Trading Corporation (TTC) was organized in 1951, following Orvis Nelson's participation in a class in international trade at Lt. General Barton K. Younts' American Institute of Foreign Trade at Thunderbird Field, Phoenix. In typical Nelson fashion, he hired the entire class of fifteen students, including the instructor, to form another Transocean subsidiary to develop a world trade organization.

The trading division was split into the Pacific Rim, under the direction of H.B. Obermiller and

Harold Hudson, director of Transocean Engineering Corporation. RL

Dick Derr; and the New York-Atlantic-European sphere, with Allan Barrie, George Nikolashin, and Stanley Rose at its helm. Another principal in the operation was Otto Reinertsen. Offices were established in New York, Geneva, London, Paris, Rome, Beirut, Asmara, Djakarta, Tokyo, Okinawa, Caracas, Baghdad, and Honolulu. At these points, agents approached foreign governments, manufacturers, exporters, importers, and merchandising agencies to find and develop markets on a global scale.

TTC was composed of five distinct operations: The International Grill Room restaurant; Travis AFB Corrosion Control, an operation which washed, shined and gave spot corrosion control to MATS aircraft ranging from twin-engined planes to the giant C-124 Globemasters; Wake Island PX and Cocktail lounge; TAL Chemical Company (Talchem), and Taloa Motors, Inc., at Guam.

Another TAL subsidiary, **TALOA Printing Company**, originally had just two employees at its inception—Charles W. Smith and Olleta Lowe. It was established to handle the corporation's printing jobs. Facilities were gradually increased and additional employees hired as the print shop took on commercial printing jobs. The shop's equipment included a complete photographic laboratory, color presses, contact printers, bindery, vari-typers, and large stocks of paper to handle any kind of printing assignment.

Richard Derr, director of Taloa Trading Company. HGE

Transocean Engineering Corporation at work. HGE

Allan A. Barrie, director of Taloa Trading, AED. HGE

-116-

Loree Strickland, of Taloa Trading Company, at San Francisco Gift Show. HGE

International Grill Room

The International Grill Room at the Oakland International Airport was managed by Pat O'Regan, from Shannon, Ireland, beginning in 1950. Paul Norville, chef for the popular restaurant and coffee shop, won four prizes at the East Bay's annual exhibition of catering arts held by the International Stewards and Caterers Association in 1951, including the Grand Award for Overall Display. The restaurant also provided frozen food services for the inflight meals of several major airlines and the Military Air Transport Service at Travis AFB and Hickam Field, Honolulu.

TAL Chemical Company (TALCHEM), was headed by Lloyd F. Coates. Founded in 1951, the company had offices and a warehouse in San Lorenzo, California, and distributed worldwide Victory Brand Chemicals and Cleaning Compounds manufactured by the Jackson Chemical Company of Los Angeles. It also had a franchise to distribute for Wyandotte Chemicals in certain foreign countries as well as domestically.

Air Activities, Inc., in 1952, under the direction of Duane R. Strand, fulfilled contracts with the U.S. State Department to spray 1,000 square miles of agricultural land in twelve Middle East countries. That year, the TAL subsidiary was asked by the Technical Cooperation Administration of the State Department to mobilize a group of American pilots to bring a speedy halt to one of the worst locust plagues the Middle East had ever experienced. From nine to twenty aircraft were used in spraying operations between 1952 and 1955. As in biblical times, the locusts moved with devastating speed and were swarming unchecked through Ethiopia, Yemen, Saudi Arabia, Jordan, Syria, Egypt, Iraq, Afghanistan, Pakistan, and India. In a counter-attack, Air Activities' pilots positioned their aircraft ahead of the locusts so as to encircle the charging pests, spraying insecticide on billions of the insects and their breeding grounds. The successful operation restored more than 672,000 acres of food-producing land to the farmers of the Middle East. The natives regarded the duster pilots as "miracle men of the sky" and traveled miles to watch them in action.

Holly Equipment Corporation was a wholly owned subsidiary of Transocean and operated profitably under a continuing lease agreement with **Western Sky Industries** (another TAL subsidiary) for the use of its facilities at Hayward Airport at Hayward, California. Western Sky was established in 1952 when TAL was awarded a Douglas Aircraft Company subcontract for an amount in excess of $3.5 million for the manufacture of aircraft components. Housed in the newly built Holly Building, named for Nelson's daughter Holly, Western Sky Industries assembled 931 wing-sections for the AD-4, AD-5, and AD-6 Sky Raider, the propeller driven multi-purpose Douglas Attack bomber of the U. S. Navy. In 1955, the company assembled forward fuselage sections of the Douglas built AD-3 Sky Warrior, a U.S. jet bomber. Western Sky's executive staff included President Ray T. Elsmore, Vice President Elon Brown, Treasurer Robert E. Hilliard and Secretary S. McKee Mhoon. The company employed about 400 workers (with a $1.2 million dollar annual payroll) in its ultra-modern 60,000 square foot facility with its high intensity lighting, monorails, and other aircraft production requirements.

When United Air Lines announced in 1947 that it was relinquishing its contract with the Navy for the operation of the **Landing Aids Experiment Station** at Arcata, California, Transocean immediately contacted the Navy and was awarded a contract to operate the station effective at midnight, February 1, 1947. The LAES was jointly sponsored by the U.S. Army, U.S. Navy, the Civil Aeronautics Administration, the Civil Aeronautics Board, the Air Transport Association, and the Air Line Pilots' Association. The project included the testing and development of high-intensity runway and approach lights, fog dispersal systems, ground controlled approach and instrument landing systems. As a result of these tests, the sponsoring agencies were able to determine, under scientifically controlled conditions, the most practical and efficient combination of aids to effect a safe all-weather landing system. Transocean was commended many times by the U.S. Navy for its management of the Arcata project.

Another of Nelson's enterprises was **The Industrial Development Divison** (under the direction of S. McKee Mhoon), which had a fully equipped plant for the manufacture of both aviation and non-aviation-related projects. They produced aircraft components for Navy fighters, chairs, and even developed two types of small refrigerators. One of these refrigerators was round and designed for use in doctors' offices and clinics, where it was necessary to store serums, vaccines, and antibiotics in small vials and containers. It had a rotating shelf on a central spindle—rather like a Lazy Susan. The second refrigerator was a junior-sized box to sell for use in small apartments or motels where space was limited.

Orvis Nelson managed to get a slice of almost every kind of business around—including a barber shop and a broom factory. Strange goings-on for an airline, according to some of Transocean's competitors. But Nelson was a man ahead of his time; the diversification of Transocean Air Lines was the forerunner of the modern business conglomerates.

Often perceived as a hard-hitting, no nonsense business man, Nelson also had an altruistic side that often cropped up—especially in hiring those who were considered "black sheep" in aviation—but also in the expansion of Transocean Air Lines.

For example, he opened the **Arrowhead Broom Factory** to provide employment for people in his home town in Minnesota. After all, Nelson reasoned, brooms were an item every household needed. The broom factory soon supplied four of the largest wholesalers in the Minneapolis area, and sales figures for 1954 showed an increase of 70 percent over 1953. Soon after, however, the operation began to lose money and eventually closed.

Nelson also took over the barbershop at the Oakland Airport terminal building—perhaps to ensure that his executives were always well groomed—and hired "Tonsorial Expert Supreme" Johnny Guerra to run the place. It was touted in the local newspaper in 1951 as a "Brand Spanking New Modern Three Chair Barber Shop."

Who would have guessed, back in 1946 when Transocean Air Lines first began traversing the airways, that the world's largest "non-sked" would someday also operate a broom factory and a "clip" joint?

Orvis Nelson anticipating a delicious lobster dinner to be prepard by the International Grill Room's award-winning chef, Paul Norville, as restaurant manager. Pat O'Regan assists. Oakland, California. AH

Paul Norville, chef at the International Grill Room, with his "Around the World With Transocean" prize winning cake. AH

Lloyd Coates, president of Transocean Air Lines Chemical Company (TALCHEM). RL

Air Activities crop dusting aircraft spraying locusts in the Middle East. HGE

Western Sky Industries plant, Hayward, California. RL

Employees of TAL subsidiary Western Sky Industries, Hayward, California. RL

A center wing assembly being readied for shipment from Western Sky Industries to Douglas Aircraft Company, El Segundo, California. RL

Taloa Motors, Okinawa. HGE

TAL's Jim Kelly makes a sale at Taloa Motors, Okinawa. HGE

Taloa Motors Gas Station at Okinawa. HGE

Landing Aids Experiment Station's all weather flying center (Arcata, California), TB-17G-100-VE, 44-85607, TALOA insignia on fin. Photo taken at San Francisco International Airport, 1947. WTL

Chapter Eight: End of a Golden Age
The Legacy of Transocean Air Lines

Strong Headwinds

"THE GOLDEN Age of Flying" was the ten years following World War II. That is how those airmen who remained in aviation during that period refer to it with certain nostalgia and affection. Orvis Nelson and his Transocean team would be among those fliers who would refer to it so, even though that era was not without its bitter experiences.

Despite fourteen years of remarkable accomplishments and the phenomenal growth of Transocean Air Lines, Nelson was never able to obtain the certification, financial backing, or aircraft necessary for the airline's expansion into the jet age. Therefore, the prospects for a happy ending looked bleak to this twentieth century adventure story.

Transocean and other supplemental airlines found themselves in a Catch-22 situation in the 1950s. Without the blessing of the CAB, they lacked respectability in the eyes of the financiers, and consequently the financiers would withhold an infusion of capital. But on the other hand, the CAB would not provide that respectability unless the airlines were well financed.

One of the ironies in the story is that Transocean itself was never subsidized by the government as were some well-known and established airlines. Rather, it relied on personal and bank financing, which was often difficult to obtain.

Support for Transocean came from many quarters in the private sector, but all of it fell on deaf ears at the CAB. When Transocean requested the right to operate across the Pacific as a certificated airline, the Honorable John J. Allen, Jr. of California twice pleaded Transocean's case before the 83rd Congress of the United States, Second Session.

On May 19, 1954, Allen included in his remarks to the Congress a review of the book, *Transocean, the Story of an Unusual Airline*, written by Richard Thruelsen, a senior editor of the Saturday Evening Post. The book review was written by Professor Bradley Jones, head of the Department of Aeronautics of the University of Cincinnati, and published in U.S. Air Services, April 1954:

"This country needs the know-how, the spirit, the courage, the ingenuity, and the resourcefulness of men like Orvis Nelson and his associates in Transocean. On March 19, 1954, Assistant Chief Examiner Wrenn, of the Civil Aeronautics Board, recommended that Transocean receive a certificate to transport persons and property between the United States and points in the Pacific Ocean areas. If this recommendation is favorably acted upon, this great non-subsidized airline will have a further opportunity to contribute to the national defense and to the advancement of our Nation's air transport industry."

On July 22, 1954, Representative Allen introduced into the Congressional Record an editorial from the Oakland Tribune which read in part:

"...the line (Transocean) is now asking for the right to operate across the Pacific as a certificated airline. That operation would be in competition with the two airlines now certified for regular operations, but there are several distinctive circumstances in Transocean's planned operations that make it an aerial trailblazer in a still different direction.

"Transocean, in asking for the right to compete in the certificated Pacific route, from Oakland to Honolulu, Guam, Wake, Manila, and Hong Kong, has pledged not to seek one cent from the United States Government for mail pay or subsidy. That is in contrast to the minimum of $6 million a year asked by one of the two competitors in its application for a renewal.

"Transocean is not opposing renewal of the application for the other line. It is asking only that the recommendation made by the examiner for the

February 3, 1950

FORTNIGHT
THE NEWSMAGAZINE OF CALIFORNIA

ORVIS NELSON
OF TRANSOCEAN AIRLINES

Orvis Nelson featured on the cover of *Fortnight*, the newsmagazine of California, February 3, 1950.

EVERY TWO WEEKS
$3.00 the year

15¢

FEBRUARY 3, 1950
(Vol. 8 • No. 3)

Group photo of Transocean Air Lines employees, circa 1953. RL

Martin 202, Oakland, 1951. Commercial Air Movement (CAM) Contract. WTL

Civil Aeronautics Bureau that it be certified for irregular service, without subsidy, but depending upon its own skill, knowledge, ability, and administrative organization to pay the way, and be given final approval by the CAB. It is an application that should be granted, without delay and without quibble."

Western Aviation in its March 1955 issue, made the following comments:

"Transocean Air Lines announced full scale continuation of all of its air and ground operations in California and throughout the world under its restricted authority as a Large Irregular Carrier and the launching of an appeal to the White House and Congress for a reversal of orders denying its certification to operate non-subsidized scheduled passenger and freight service between Oakland, Burbank, Hawaii, and the Orient.

"These steps were taken in the wake of the issuance of a White House directive requesting the Civil Aeronautics Board to deny the war and airline veterans'-founded California airline's application for certification in the West Coast-Hawaii and transpacific certificate renewal cases."

Commenting on the unprecendented White House action by President Eisenhower in the cases, Transocean's executive vice president Sam Wilson said: "If the announced intended action is carried through, the Civil Aeronautics Board will have preserved its dubious record of never having issued a new major route certificate in all its sixteen year history and also will have protected from competition the subsidized carriers which were blanketed in under the grandfather's rights of 1938."

Reorganization

In October 1955, the board of directors and a majority of the stockholders of Transocean Air Lines approved a plan of reorganization of the company's corporate structure. Essentially an air carrier regulated by the CAB, Transocean had engaged for some years in non-air carrier aeronautical activities and other activities that were only remotely connected with aviation. TAL was also the parent company of subsidiaries engaged in both aeronautical and non-aeronautical activities. The purposes of the plan were defined to the stockholders as the following:

1. To simplify administrative controls, accounting procedures, and reporting practices.
2. To divide into separate corporations certain activities previously administered as divisional activities.
3. To revive a dormant corporation now wholly owned by the company and assign divisional activities to it.
4. To provide a basis for future financing for the parent or subsidiary companies to best serve the interests of the stockholders and the public.

Transocean Air Lines changed its name to The Transocean Corporation of California, effective June 1, 1956.

New Investors

After the reorganization of TAL in 1956, R. Stanley Dollar, of the Dollar Steamship Line (who had been involved financially with TAL as early as 1952), lent $500,000 to the ailing Transocean and agreed to finance a fleet of aircraft in exchange for a large block of stock. But before that deal could be completed, Dollar backed out in early 1957.

Shortly thereafter, Nelson's own lawyer informed him that the Atlas Corporation, a Wall Street investment company, might be willing to provide the needed financing. When Nelson demurred, saying he was not impressed by the people who managed Atlas, the lawyer produced a handful of documents, threw them down on Nelson's desk and told him that he had no choice. The documents showed that through purchases and proxies the Atlas Corporation had acquired forty percent of Transocean's stock.

To attempt to explain the circumstances leading up to this point in Transocean's history, it is necessary to return briefly to earlier years and instances.

In July 1946, Transocean had filed an application with the CAB for certification as a supplemental carrier, along with several hundred other small airlines, started during that same period. By January 1958, only a few carriers remained, including TAL. Nearly all had ceased operations after twelve years. They had all flown under the dark cloud that their authority to operate could be canceled on thirty days notice by the CAB.

Finally, in January 1950, Transocean received a five-year certificate as a supplemental carrier for domestic and overseas operations. This limited and temporary authority made public financing impossible. Nelson continued through the years to investigate the possibilities of private financing which ultimately led to the agreement with the Atlas Corporation of July 1957.

The original agreement between Transocean and Atlas called for Atlas to sell the Babb Company, an Atlas subsidiary, to Transocean Corporation of California. Atlas, in return, would receive Transocean stock, would assist in the financing of a minimum fleet of six large aircraft of the Super Constellation type, and would further assist in raising a large amount of working capital. CAB approval of the agreement was necessary because Atlas owned a controlling interest in Northeast Airlines. According to Nelson, it was probably Atlas's control of Northeast that caused or at least contributed to the long delay in processing the case by the CAB.

There was a remarkable amount of intrigue surrounding the entire affair. R.E.G. Davies, Curator of Air Transport, National Air and Space Museum at the Smithsonian Institution in Washington, D.C., effectively sums up the raiding of Transocean in his book, *Rebels and Reformers of the Airways*, in these excerpts from the chapter titled, "Orvis Nelson—Mr. Transocean":

"...Interference with management and the consequent loss of some good executives forced Nelson to ask for a new agreement with Atlas, which on November 20, 1958, turned over to (Floyd) Odlum's corporation almost all of the Transocean organization except the airline itself.

"By the time the CAB approved the amended Atlas Agreement, Transocean was only a shadow of its former self. Under the insidious influence of Atlas, which was aided consciously or unconsciously, by the CAB's agonizing delay in making decisions, Transocean just fell apart, deprived as it was of its affiliated maintenance, manufacturing, and construction companies through the Atlas deal.

"The treatment of Transocean by the government agency was a travesty of justice. The CAB seems to have carried out a policy of deliberate extermination by procrastination, following the blueprint supplied in a memorandum dated September 16, 1948, written by its chief of the Bureau of Economic Regulations, Louis W. Goodkind, who was far from being either good or kind to the nonscheduled airlines. He outlined ways in which their attempts to attain legitimacy in the eyes of the board could be thwarted, and the board's treatment of Transocean was a textbook case."

The memorandum Davies refers to would eventually serve as a requiem to Nelson's bold vision and Transocean's pioneering contributions to international aviation, both military and commercial.

TAL switchboard operators. HGE

TAL-AEMCO guards, left to right: Fred Burbank, Tommy Dee, Art Kern, Frank Foutch, Frank Kephart, Earl B. Brennecke and Walt Thomas. HGE

Sherwood Nichols pulling the props through, Harmon Field, Guam, 1948. RL

Signing up for the AEMCO Red Sox baseball team, Frank Halsell, back row, right. Others unidentified. AH

Receiving commendation certificates for outstanding job performance from Douglass Johnson, back row, left to right: Alburta Knupfer, Douglass Johnson, unidentified, Mike Lewis, Dutch Hasskamp, unidentified. Front row: Ray Foster, H. "Ole" Olesten, unidentified. HOP

Martin 202, Oakland, 1951. WTL

TAL DC-4 N9940F, Oakland, 1954. WTL

Martin 202, Oakland, California, 1951. WTL

Martin 202 at John Rogers Airport, Honolulu, Hawaii. Left to right: Christopher Angelos, Carlos Mathias, Doug Cole, Bill Murray and Bob Edgerly. NE

At Hangar 5, left to right: Paul Dutter (PAL), Captain Bill Word, Guard Guy Rencher, others unidentified. AH

Robert Lang, chief engineer AEMCO.

George Mourgas, TAL station manager, Oakland, California. RL

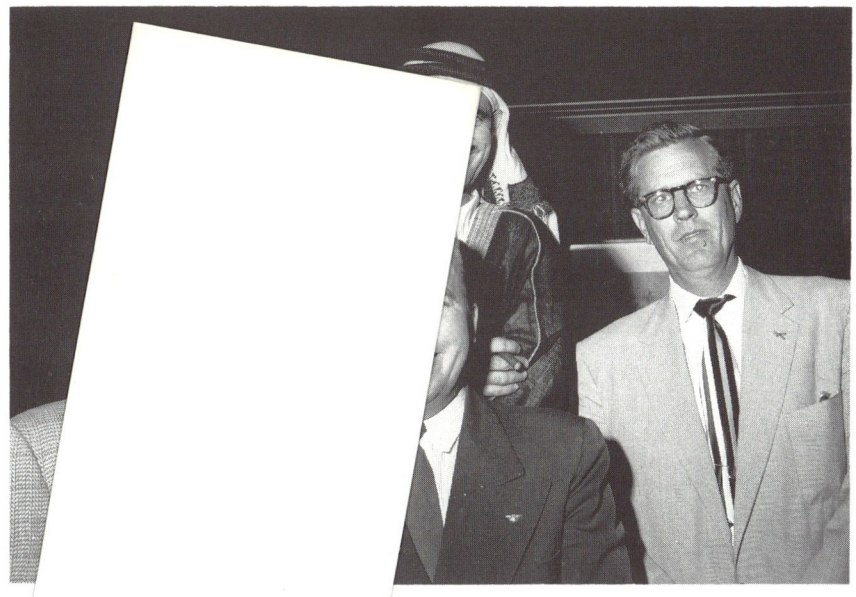

Left to right: Ray Foster, Bill Benge and Don McAfee. The "Sheik" is radio operator Ralph Lewis, 1953. RL

8,

Fer-

ara front nor el, Mar- eu oyd, Ruth own are Pat eiros, sen and

RL

TAL's "Southern Squadron," the sales staff at Los Angeles. Left to right, front row: Dottie Nomura, Marion Tan, Donna Rieff and Laura Olson. Left to right, back row: Gerald Orlin, Fred Berg, William Hartney, Wendell Moen and Robert Weeks. Not shown are Max Hodder, Newell Davis, Art Osyman, Bob Arndt and Colin Kennedy. HF

Luncheon meeting, Alameda, California. Left to right: unidentified, Vivian Sims, Dwight Mefford, Esther Lavagnini, Don McAfee, next three unidentified, Esther McConnell, Jim Corbett, Claude Turner, Bill Wilson, Ray Foster, Bill Benge, Vi Corrington, Frank Soares, unidentified and H. "Ole" Olesten. RL

Beginning of the End

Despite Nelson's valiant and persistent efforts to keep the airline flying, and the purchase of fourteen Stratocruisers in 1957 from British Overseas Airways (BOAC), the end was in sight by late 1958. The inability of the airline to obtain the certification to fly specified routes and into specified markets was unquestionably the root of the problem. Nelson's persuasive charm was ineffective at the CAB, as was that of industrialist and resort builder Henry J. Kaiser at the Honolulu hearing of the CAB's Transpacific Case in 1959. Kaiser rocked the hearing room with ten pages of commercial developments being planned that cried out for more air transport[ation] with designated routes between the fiftieth state and the mainland, and even beyond Hawaii. He unveiled plans for building 5,000 hotel rooms and a resort city on 6,000 acres of land at the eastern end of Oahu.

Kaiser gave nine reasons for the need for additional air service to the Hawaiian Islands. He also predicted an increase to one million tourists a year (a nearly four-fold increase) to Hawaii by the late sixties. He foresaw that within ten years tourism would be the Islands' number one industry. He put forth in convincing terms that "the dynamic power of free competition unleashed through the certification of additional competitive airlines would result in vastly increased travel to Hawaii." He concluded, "We sadly need—we badly need more air transportation."

The cross-examination by Pan Am's Elihu Schoot was intended to develop the argument that Pan Am and United should be given a chance to show that they could handle the expected increase in traffic to the islands. Witness Kaiser bluntly replied, "The traffic should NOT be left in your hands—at any rate. That is not free enterprise."

Near the end of 1959, Transocean was in its final days and in need of financial life-support systems. But there were none available. Now owing an enormous amount to the Internal Revenue Service for unpaid taxes and in debt to its suppliers, the airline was on the verge of collapse. After several major oil companies revoked the airline's credit for fuel, the aircraft were grounded one by one as they returned to Oakland. Cash became unavailable, and even flight captains and other employees who had only recently financed the purchase of gasoline with their own money, could no longer do so. On one occasion, a Transocean captain borrowed a passenger's credit card to buy fuel to continue a flight when he found out his TAL credit card had been canceled due to non-payment. The passenger was reimbursed by the airline, but the story made news in *Time* magazine. Paychecks were missed, and employees at headquarters in Oakland and those stationed overseas were getting nervous.

Transocean's Complete Pacific Schedules
Now Appearing in the Official Airline Guide

"ROYAL HAWAIIAN" service to Hawaii in luxurious new SUPER CONSTELLATIONS . . . reserved seating in deep-cushioned reclinable lounge chairs.

"ROYAL PACIFICAN" service to Okinawa in pressurized Constellations, superbly air-conditioned, complimentary meals, 66-lb. baggage allowance.

COMPLETE CONSTELLATION SCHEDULES BETWEEN
U.S.-HAWAII-ORIENT*

WESTBOUND: PACIFIC COAST—HAWAII—ORIENT

Read Down	Mon	Tue	Tue	Tue	Wed	Thu	Thu	Fri	Sat	Sun
WESTBOUND	301	102	302	502		104	504	305		107
LOS ANGELES .... Lv (Burbank Airport)	11 00	↓	11 00	18 00			18 00	23 45		
OAKLAND Lv		11 00		22 00 Wed		11 00	22 00 Fri	↓ Sat		11 00
HONOLULU .... Ar	17 30	17 00	17 30	04 00		17 00	04 00	06 15		17 00
HONOLULU Lv				07 00 Thu			07 00 Sat			
WAKE .... Ar				14 00	↓ Fri		14 00			
						↓ Sun				
WAKE Lv				15 30	P06 45	J04 45	15 30			
GUAM .... Ar				19 40			19 40			
GUAM Lv				21 00			21 00			
OKINAWA .... Ar				01 45 Fri			01 45 Sun			
	Sat·	Fri						Mon	Sun	Tue
OKINAWA Lv	J03 30	C21 05		C06 15			C06 15	N19 05	C21 05	J03 30
TAIPEI .... Ar				C07 40			C07 40			
TAIPEI Lv			C08 00	C09 00			C09 00	↓		
HONG KONG .... Ar				C12 00			C12 00			
MANILA .... Ar			C12 10					N21 49		
FUKUOKA .... Ar	J06 30									J06 30
OSAKA .... Ar	J09 50	Sat			Fri	Sun			Mon	J09 50
TOKYO .... Ar	J12 00	C01 50			P12 15	J10 00			C01 50 Tue	J12 00
SEOUL .... Ar		C13 00							C13 00	

J—Japan Airlines. N—Northwest Airlines. C—Civil Air Transport. Italics—Connecting carrier to/from Burbank. *—Connecting carrier between Okinawa and Orient Cities.
Flight 301 Effective April 28th; Flight 102 Effective May 6th—operates on alternate weeks; Flight 104 Effective May 1st. Flights 502 and 504 not available to local boarding passengers to Honolulu. Flight 302 Effective May 13th operates on alternate weeks.

EASTBOUND: ORIENT—HAWAII—PACIFIC COAST

Read Down	Sun	Sun	Mon	Tue	Tue	Wed	Thu	Fri	Sat	Sat
EASTBOUND	207	607	401	202	402		204		606	406
SEOUL Lv			Sat C14 00 Sun					Thu C14 00 Fri		
TOKYO Lv	Sat J21 30		00 01				Fri J15 00	Fri J21 30	C00 01	
OSAKA Lv							J17 20			
FUKUOKA Lv							J20 50			
MANILA Lv				Sun N08 30						Fri C13 10
HONG KONG Lv		C13 30					↓		Fri C13 30	
TAIPEI .... Ar		C16 25							C16 25	C17 10
TAIPEI Lv		C17 30					Sat		C17 30	←
OKINAWA .... Ar		C20 35	C05 30	N12 49			J00 10		C20 35 Sat	
OKINAWA Lv		23 00 Mon							01 00	
GUAM .... Ar		05 45							07 45	
GUAM Lv	Sun	07 05					Sat		09 05	
WAKE .... Ar	J07 20	15 15					J07 20		17 15	
WAKE Lv	→	16 45							18 45	
HONOLULU .... Ar		03 45							05 45	
HONOLULU Lv	21 15 Mon	08 00	21 15	21 15 Wed	21 15		21 15 Fri		09 00	10 00 ↓
OAKLAND .... Ar	09 10	20 00		09 15			09 15		21 00	
LOS ANGELES .... Ar (Burbank Airport)		22 37	Tue 09 45		Wed 09 45					21 30

J—Japan Airlines. N—Northwest Airlines. C—Civil Air Transport. Italics—Connecting carrier from/to Burbank. *—Connecting carrier between Okinawa and Orient Cities.
Flight 401 Effective April 28th; Flight 202 Effective May 6th—operates on alternate weeks; Flight 204 Effective May 1st; Flights 606 and 607 are not available to local boarding passengers from Hawaii; Flight 402 Effective May 6th operates on alternate weeks.

TRANSOCEAN AIR LINES — America's Foremost Supplemental Air Carrier

April 1958

A Personal Account

Captain E.M. "Red" Wickkiser was based in Iran when rumors about the company being in trouble began to surface (as far back as 1952 and 1953). He recalls one of the several occasions which most Transocean employees also well remember and which serves to highlight Nelson's charisma.

"Our pay was late, and we were 12,000 miles from the home office and could get no confirmation of anything except that we weren't being paid. At this time, Iranair had six DC-3s, and we were just getting by on our local cost of living allowance. We were about to revolt, to shut down the operation. Why work with no pay when we didn't know what was going on? Don McAfee was the general manager at the time, and he did the best he could, but he couldn't get our money for us. He did tell us, however, that Orvis was on one of his round-the-world swings and was to stop in Teheran and that he would have answers to our questions.

"By the time Orvis arrived, feelings were running high. We were all invited to drinks and canapes at McAfee's home where Orvis started with the history of Transocean and went on to Japan Air Lines, Lufthansa, Air Jordan, and Air Djibouti—plus the plans of expansion, the eventual combining of routes of all the airlines to be a truly global airline to compete with Pan American.

"He promised to pay us immediately, even told us where the money was coming from. And the expressions on the faces of the employees changed from glowering rebelliousness to smiles.

"We still didn't have the money owed us, but Orvis had charmed us to the point of believing, and certainly we soon did have our money. Orvis could come in, read our attitudes, and satisfy us with his explanations, but particularly with his charm."

End of a Dream

When Transocean ceased operations in bankruptcy in 1960, the papers filed with the bankruptcy court contained the technical and financial reasons but still did not explain the complete story, which had to do with forces within and without the airline. It had to do with the unending quest for certification and the seemingly indifferent—and even antagonistic—federal bureaucracy, rich but overcautious merchant banks, and apprehensive aircraft manufacturers. Within the airline, it had to do with the character and personality of a visionary leader and his reflection on his totally loyal but totally unquestioning administrative staff.

Those who are gifted with creative and leader-

Francis Jones, treasurer, Transocean Air Lines. AH

ship abilities, who build dreams into large organizations, are sometimes brought down by those same characteristics that made them successful. Their unbridled enthusiasm and fearlessness, their single mindedness, idealism, and self-confidence: all these qualities equip them for victory. But at times these charismatic leaders are overly idealistic, and often unwise in their judgements of other people.

There were those who believed that Orvis Nelson, the founder, president, and continuing force of Transocean was just such a man. While his accomplishments have already been recorded, there are those who suggested that these qualities led to the company's resources being spread too thin by over-diversification. Others felt that Nelson's weakness was that he was too trusting of certain members of his staff, that he delegated an excessive amount of authority to them, and that he failed to insist on more efficient bookkeeping methods.

Many believed there were political machinations at work behind the scenes that effectively blocked Transocean from securing the new Boeing 707 jets that the airline needed urgently to enter the jet age in the Pacific. A former officer of the airline recalls that Transocean had negotiated with Boeing to buy three 707s—two of which Cubana had on order from Boeing, but canceled when the Cuban government fell before their delivery. Boeing was anxious to sell, and Transocean began negotiations involving the manufacturer, Japan Air Lines, and some banking institutions for the acquisition of the three 707s. To generate the capital for their purchase, Transocean planned to charter two of them to Japan Air Lines for two years because JAL was extremely anxious to beat Pan American in the Pacific with the first jet aircraft. Japan Air Lines agreed to guarantee payments to the lending institutions, and entered into an agreement with Transocean for a back-to-back lease of the aircraft until the delivery of its own DC-8 aircraft from Douglas. The third 707 was to be used by Transocean for its own charter flights if the deal was consummated.

There was evidence to suggest that one of the major scheduled airlines pressured Boeing Aircraft Company not to sell the aircraft to Transocean, with the implied threat that if they did so, their company would not buy any jet aircraft from Boeing. This alleged conspiracy became the basis of a $199 million restraint of trade suit against Boeing and the parties named in the legal action. The suit contended that the defendants blocked TAL's purchase of three Boeing planes and interfered with its re-financing program. San Francisco lawyer Joe Alioto, an antitrust specialist, accepted the case. But during the early phase of the proceedings, Mr. Alioto campaigned for the office of mayor of San Francisco and won. The case was prepared and tried in court, not by Mr. Alioto, but by his associates in his law firm.

When the verdict was pronounced, it was against Transocean. It was a crushing loss, and observers within Transocean felt that had Joe Alioto tried the case, the airline would have won. There was recourse, however, and that recourse was to appeal to a higher court. But no one from TAL had the $30,000 for the transcripts from the trial, much less the filing fee for a new trial. (Trans International Airline would be the first non-scheduled airline with a jet in its fleet—one of the earlier DC-8s—late in 1963)

In the meantime, the corporate life of Transocean became more critical every day. But as late as January 15, 1960, Nelson was still optimistic about keeping Transocean in business despite what he termed another major setback. The following is excerpted from a letter he sent to stockholders of The Transocean Corporation of California on that date:

"...This setback was triggered in August 1959 by a misleading press dispatch from Washington, D.C. concerning CAB approval for the agreement between Transocean and the Atlas Corporation. The dispatch stated in part '...the CAB today approved control (by Atlas) of Northeast Airlines and Transocean Air Lines...' Actually, the agreement approved by the Civil Aeronautics Board allowed Transocean Corporation of California to sell to the Atlas Corporation its aircraft maintenance and non-flying companies. Transocean, in return was relieved of a substantial amount of indebtedness and received a twenty percent interest in a new corporation, called International Aviation Services, to be formed by merging the Babb Company, an aircraft brokerage firm owned by Atlas, with Transocean's companies. Transocean Corporation of California would retain Transocean Air Lines as its major operating entity. The 'control' aspects of the approved agreement referred only to long term debt to the Atlas Corporation which remained after the closing in August 1959. Transocean had up to five years to liquidate this obligation."

Nelson went on to explain that Transocean creditors who had carried substantial debts during the months the CAB was considering the case were startled by the erroneous announcement, and many moved quickly to collect. This caused a run on the company's funds which was complicated by delays in receipt of regular funds in transit. TAL fell behind in its payrolls and tax payments, as well as other obligations. The management of the airline had to decide whether to liquidate or stay in business. Liquidating meant that the company's 1,200 employees would be thrown out of work, the stockholders' investment would be lost, and that the creditors would have to take substantial losses.

He said that Transocean management was convinced that the interests of all concerned could be best served by continuing in business. They thought that by continuing operations, the airline had a reasonable chance for a successful recovery from its difficulties.

The overwhelming majority of the employees, he noted, had immediately pledged their support, and he had been able to assure the stockholders that an agreement for deferred payments had been worked out with the company's major creditors. He reminded them that operations during August and September of 1959 were generating more than $1.5 million each month and that conservative projections indicated that earnings could continue at a rate that would permit normal operations once the financial difficulties were overcome. A $500,000 bank loan had also been arranged to assist in meeting the most pressing cash problems.

Nelson's January 15, 1960 letter to the stockholders ended with the encouraging statement that a refinancing program for Transocean, one that seemed promising, was being studied by a leading New York financial institution. He expressed the hope that the long-awaited unlimited certificate authorizing Transocean as the third unrestricted carrier in the Pacific would be forthcoming—a hope that was doomed even as Nelson signed his name at the bottom of his letter to the Transocean stockholders.

But every one of Nelson's heroic last-ditch efforts failed to save the airline. The death blow was dealt by the airline's insurance company when it canceled the company's insurance policy. Without that coverage, the airplanes could not fly. On a chilly morning in January 1960, the last Stratocruiser flown by Transocean Air Lines landed at the Oakland International Airport where the rest of the once proud fleet was already grounded. And Transocean Air Lines folded its wings forever.

By October 1961, most of TAL's remaining equipment was liquidated for $60,000 at a bankruptcy sale. The company had previously sold aircraft worth some $14 million for $105,000 to satisfy four creditors. At involuntary bankruptcy proceedings, officials revealed that Transocean owed a total of $13,962,000 to some 1,200 creditors. The Internal Revenue Service also wanted the back taxes owed by Transocean. However, the bankruptcy court had been assured by Nelson that a majority of the creditors, in number and amount, had accepted a plan to arrange for payment of debts in a legal document already presented to the bankruptcy court.

According to a newspaper account of those proceedings, Transocean's attorney, Maxwell Newmark, said that all that would be needed to put the airline on an operational basis was consent by three states to a plan for delayed payment of back taxes. Three other states had already agreed. Newmark said that under the plan presented to the bankruptcy court, a new corporation had been formed to supply initial financial support at a minimum of $250,000 and provide any further money needed.

Transocean's newest financial angel, The Rhone Company, which had been incorporated in Nevada, was backed by unnamed Eastern capitalists. Transocean would, in effect, become a subsidiary of Rhone, but would continue to fly under its own name, reactivating its routes to the Pacific islands and Europe. Newmark said he had been advised that Transocean's rights to do so were still valid under authority of the Civil Aeronautics Board.

But again the airline's hopes were dashed by a lack of enthusiasm from the U.S. Government. This became patently clear after Assistant U.S. Attorney General Thomas A. Kennelly revealed that a letter received by him from the U.S. Controller stated, "...we are not aware of any vital necessity to revive this carrier's operation."

The reason, Kennelly said, was that the government currently had a claim of $590,978 against Transocean, not including $150,000 owed the Internal Revenue Service, and was not anxious to risk incurring heavier claims.

Nelson and hundreds of loyal employees reeled under the devastating defeat as did his wife, Edith and his family. The blows were personal and financial. But Nelson's Norwegian upbringing, his stubbornness, and his love of aviation would not permit him to abandon his dream. He was down but not out. He would continue to try to resurrect Transocean Air Lines.

Finally, in 1965 a $42 million damage suit was filed on behalf of bankrupt Transocean against Atlas Corporation of New York. The suit charged fraud and misrepresentation on the part of Atlas in its financial dealings with Transocean. The charges concerned Atlas's acquisition of capital for TAL to purchase pressurized aircraft.

The complaint against Atlas was brought by Federal Bankruptcy Trustees, not TAL, appointed to oversee the affairs of Transocean and its parent corporation, Transocean Corporation of California. It stated that Atlas had "assumed direction and control of Transocean's operations and through mismanagement drove Transocean into bankruptcy." The complaint asked for $27 million general and compensatory damages and $15 million punitive damages. The verdict was once more against Transocean.

Nelson Never Gives Up

During the 1960s, Orvis and Edie Nelson moved to Europe where Nelson started a new company, Air Systems. Based in Copenhagen, Air Systems employed three flight crews. Among them were former TAL employees Don McAfee, Ed Landwehr, and Jesse Morrison. The airline transported cattle and race horses in C-74 transports by night throughout Europe and Asia.

Nelson had purchased seven of the C-74s in Arizona, along with the spare parts. The huge transports could carry sixty cows or sixty-eight horses, and each one had an elevator in the center section of the fuselage to allow access for the livestock. Air Systems lasted for about one year. The end came soon after a newly hired pilot crashed a cattle-loaded C-74 five feet from the top of a mountain at Marseilles, France. The law suits that followed proved too much for the struggling young company.

Now Nelson's first concern wasn't the pursuit of capital for Transocean but for just enough money to provide for his family. Now just a pilot and not an entrepreneur, he agreed to fly one trip to Nigeria in 1966 as copilot on a DC-4 owned by an acquaintance. Legal papers and the export papers for the freight they carried had been filed in Brussels, departure point for the flight. In fact, Nelson, concerned that part of his load was guns, checked with the department of trade in Brussels to be sure everything was legal. It was.

While flying over Cameroon in West Africa, the DC-4 ran out of fuel. The flight captain had apparently neglected to bring along the proper maps and became lost. They were past the point of no return when the fuel ran out. There was no choice but to put down in a crash landing. The captain was, fortunately, unhurt, but as he had no landing permit for Cameroon, he panicked and abandoned Nelson who was trapped and injured inside the wrecked aircraft. Orvis spend five months in a local hospital and was held responsible for the landing violation as well. This left him in desperate financial straits.

Rumors that Nelson had transferred all of his wealth to his wife and mother, or that he had large sums of money in Swiss bank accounts were unfounded. These rumors were partially squelched when it became known that Edie Nelson had to borrow two hundred dollars from friends to help finance Orvis' return to the United States.

Disillusioned and weary after recovering from this latest ordeal, Nelson moved his family back to Minnesota for a few years to regain his strength and to put his life back in order. But the time came when he could no longer ignore his persistent love for aviation, and the family returned to California. There Nelson developed an aviation consulting business for several years, all the while pressing his case in Washington, D.C. at every opportunity.

Nelson had struggled for sixteen years to obtain the CAB certification which had long been denied. On October 6, 1976, he prepared what would be his last statement before the United States Senate Small Business Committee regarding the CAB transpacific renewal case, Docket 5031 et al, in a final attempt to restart Transocean. He forcefully recounted the travesty of justice wrought by the CAB upon Transocean Air Lines and other non-scheduled carriers. Yet, his concluding remarks were filled with the optimism and vitality so characteristic of the man: "...We have people standing by, many of the Transocean originals, eager to get Transocean back in the air."

Orvis Nelson was not to savor the triumph of building a new Transocean Air Lines. He died from a heart attack less than two months later, on December 2, 1976.

On October 24, 1978, eighteen years after the demise of Transocean Air Lines, President Jimmy Carter signed into law the Airline Deregulation Act. Transocean Air Lines' certificate was revoked on December 8, 1987.

TAL's Legacy

Following the 1960 bankruptcy, the people of Transocean Air Lines soon scattered to the four winds. Before the year was over, they were working for many other airlines or businesses. Some joined Air Vietnam; others flew for Air America, Lufthansa, Transamerica, or World Airways.

Global Associates, a logistics support contractor for the military, was an outgrowth of Transocean Air Lines after the failure of the company. Many of the airline's employees assumed management roles and were instrumental in the growth of the organization, which employed as many as 2,500 people. Among them were Douglass Johnson, Stan Morketter, Ray Tyrell, Glen Elkins, Gene Cohan, Don McAfee, Carl VanHecke, and Robert Lang. In December 1963, Global won a contract with the U.S. Navy to support its base on the island of Kwajalein, and in 1964 continued its services at the base after it was taken over by the U.S. Army. Global Associates is currently handling four contracts for the U.S. Navy, maintains a base at Charleston, South Carolina, to service, store, and issue U.S. Army amphibian craft, and services the inactive ("mothball") fleet of the U.S. Navy.

Western Sky Industries, formerly one of Transocean's subsidiary companies, continues in business at Hayward, California, manufacturing special aluminum aircraft fasteners and custom moulded plastic parts for the aircraft and automotive industries.

In 1960, Bill Glenn and the first thirty-five aircraft mechanics on Transocean's seniority list formed a repair station, The Hangar Four Corporation, at Oakland International, to enable them to finish out TAL's contract with Resort Air Lines. Francis Jones, who was then the treasurer of Transocean, obtained funds for the venture from the Stanley Dollar Corporation. The Hangar Four Corporation also gained as customers World Airways, Transamerica Airline, Slick, Seaboard and Western, and other commercial carriers flying to Korea. During its three years in business, thirty-five Constellations, four 1649 Constellations, twenty-four DC-4s and twelve DC-6 aircraft operated from Hangar Four Corporation's hangar.

When Transocean was clearly going out of business, thirty-three of the Transocean pilots flying for Japan Air Lines formed a new company, International Air Services (IASCO), and renegotiated the TAL contract with Japan Air Lines. Each of the pilots contributed two thousand dollars to fund the corporation. Bob Hench was elected president, and under his guidance IASCO trained Japanese pilots for Japan Airlines for both domestic and international routes. IASCO is still in business today under the leadership of Captain Jim Jack.

Many former TAL employees became successful entrepreneurs; others associated themselves with renowned institutions such as the Lawrence Laboratory at Livermore, California; several are millionaires who readily acknowledge that the experience gained working at Transocean and the contacts they made through their association with the airline contributed much to their present-day success.

It is true, as might be expected, that many of the Transocean employees were bitter when the airline went broke. Most had families and some lost not only their jobs but thousands of dollars in unpaid wages, corporate stock, or from personal loans made to the company that were never reimbursed. But time has put the issue into somewhat better perspective for most of the Transocean family. In retrospect, it is clear that no amount of money could buy the friendships they made around the world nor the remarkable experiences and memories garnered in a time they now feel was the best of their lives.

Orvis Nelson started with a dream, his only assets were a small band of enthusiastic employees who believed that nothing was impossible.

When the news spread about the crazy airline somebody named Orvis Nelson was attempting to start out at the Oakland Airport, some who worked for the elite scheduled airlines predicted that he'd never get it off the ground. "Why, Nelson hasn't even got an airplane, much less a hangar to put it in," they scoffed. The rest is history.

At its height, the Transocean organization included ten companies, making it the first aviation conglomerate. The airline itself employed 1,500 persons. Including the personnel of its subsidiary companies, the total number exceeded 6,700. Transocean's gross annual sales climbed as high as $50 million dollars. By April 1958, after twelve years of business, Transocean's aircraft had flown a total of 1,290,966,900 passenger miles, 126,990,642 cargo ton-miles, and 66,828,237 aircraft miles—the equivalent of more than 135 round-trips to the moon.

There was something indefinable, something special about Nelson and the men and women whose dedication, ingenuity, and teamwork created the world's largest supplemental air carrier. And it is through this group of unique people that the spirit of Transocean Air Lines, a truly great airline, lives on.

Transocean Air Lines' Safety Record

During almost fourteen years of continuous and concentrated aviation and airline activity, totaling in excess of 70 milion aircraft miles, more than a billion and a half passenger miles, and over 85 million cargo-ton miles (often in areas with few or non-existent navigational aids or ground installations), Transocean's total casualties were ninety passengers and sixteen crew.

Considering the pioneering nature of much of Transocean's flying, in peacetime and in war, this record alone is a measure of the unparalleled dedication to safety and service which made Transocean one of the greatest airlines—though certainly the least recognized—in U.S. air transport history.

A Transocean hope that was not to be fulfilled—an artist's rendering of a Transocean Air Lines 707 jet aircraft. HGE

Left to right: Noreen Wilson, General Douglas MacArthur, Samuel L. Wilson and Marine Lt. Victor R. Bisceglia. TAL Captain Wilson piloted the "Light of Peace" flight to obtain General MacArthur's signature for a friendship book, gift of the city of San Francisco to the school children of Japan. October 24, 1952. HGE

Fifth from left, TAL Captain Samuel L. Wilson. Second from right, Ishiji Motoki, president, Northern California Japanese Chamber of Commerce. HGE

Afterword

March 15, 1948

*T*HE DRIVER of the Key System bus pulled to the curb in front of the old terminal building at the Oakland International Airport. There was a swoosh of air as the doors swung open, and I stepped out onto the sidewalk and stood for a few minutes watching the airplanes land and take off. I was wearing a brown and white striped seersucker suit with silver buttons and a white Peter Pan collar, with matching cuffs. The skirt was straight and tight, the "new look" of 1948; its hemline reached half-way to my ankles. On my feet were brown pumps with pointed toes—fashionable, but miserably uncomfortable.

This was to be my first day at work as a junior stenographer at Transocean Air Lines. I had celebrated my eighteenth birthday in January, had recently graduated from high school, and was now on my way to an exciting career in aviation. Soon I would learn of faraway places with strange names: Djibouti, Basra, Bora Bora, Osaka. Working in the personnel office, I would learn how to process job applications and secure things called passports and visas for the handsome young pilots and other employees of the airline—for $165.00 a month salary. Perhaps now I'd also take my first flight. I was ecstatic.

A brisk breeze whipped leaves and dirt from the sidewalk into miniature whirlwinds around my legs as I began the long walk to the barracks building near the end of Earhart Drive, and what would become a lifetime love affair with Transocean Air Lines.

Walking along, I remembered the first time I had seen an airplane. I was five years old and had been sitting in the middle of a field at my grandfather's South Carolina farm making "frog houses" in the newly plowed earth by covering a bare foot with dirt, patting it firmly into place and then carefully removing my foot, creating an igloo-style house for frogs or toads in need of a place to hole up. It was then that I heard a noise in the sky that reminded me of the sound of the engine of my grandfather's Model A Ford when he cranked it up to go to town. I looked up and saw something strange silhouetted against the bright blue sky, but I wasn't frightened. Through a window I could see a man inside. The object flew over the stand of pine trees at the end of the field, becoming smaller and smaller until it finally disappeared from view. My grandfather explained that the marvelous thing I had just seen was an airplane. Now, thirteen years later, I hurried (as fast as I could in those pointy-toed shoes) to my first full-time job at an airline on the other side of the continent.

Transocean Air Lines is stamped indelibly on the hearts and lives of those of us who were fortunate enough to have been a part of those golden years from 1946 to 1960—all of us drawn to Oakland, California, and most of us destined to retain this common bond throughout our lives.

Today, over a quarter of a century after the airline's demise, nearly 500 of its former employees are members of the Taloa Alumni Association, and the numbers grow as word of the organization gets around. Seldom can a group of former employees of a defunct company match Taloans in keeping in touch with one another for so long a time. The Transocean group can be compared to an extended family as it meets for a reunion every year. The association also publishes a quarterly newsletter and has reproduced, for nostalgia's sake, one of the Transocean Air Lines' calendars featuring photographs taken during the 1940s and 1950s, winged lapel pins, window decals, and postcards showing one of Transocean's Stratocruisers.

Only a handful of the flight crew members of Transocean continue to fly for the commercial airlines, but many of those who have retired still take to the skies. Spirited and ever adventurous, nearly all of the alumni continue to travel as passengers as often as possible to faraway corners of the earth on the sleek jets of the scheduled airlines. Some own and pilot their private planes. Others, like Ed Peiffer, a retired airman in his middle seventies, get their kicks soaring in ultralight planes. And another former Transocean pilot, author Ernest K. Gann, who is now seventy-seven years of age, recently tried sky-diving. Gann said flying for fifty-three years without taking the plunge was long enough.

Those who served Transocean valiantly on the ground also still pursue life with vigor. As Sherwood Nichols has said, "You won't find many Transocean people in rocking chairs."

The esprit de corps among the people of this once great airline is as prevalent today as it was in 1946. Perhaps the words of Wally Barnett, who was a radio operator for Transocean, best sum up the feelings of most of the airlines' alumni: "We were a young, enthusiastic group, mostly straight from the military. We wanted to make our niche in the commercial aviation world. We worked, played, lived, and some died together. There was something magic about Transocean Air Lines; a magic that I haven't experienced since."

The wings are folded.

TAL's Chicago office.

Appendix

The Accomplishments of Transocean Air Lines

See text for additional information regarding some of the major accomplishments of TAL subsidiaries such as Aircraft Engineering & Maintenance Co., Oakland Aircraft Engineering Co., and Flight Enterprises.

Major Services on Behalf of the United States Government

1946 Air Transport Command, two trips per day California-Hawaii, eleven months

1947 USN AND CAA, operation Landing Aids Experiment Station, Arcata, California, three years

U.S. Army airlift, 750 military dependents Seattle-Tokyo

U.S. Army Engineers, 25,000-30,000 civilian defense workers transported to and from Pacific bases

1948 U.S. Army, 2,700 military dependents Germany-United States

U.S. Army, 700 military dependents Seattle-Tokyo

International Refugee Organization of United Nations, 25,000 war refugees Munich to Caracas, Venezuela

USAF, 100 transatlantic flights, United States-Europe, in support of the Berlin Airlift

150 C-46 aircraft ferry, United States-China

13,000 International Refugee Organization evacuees from Shanghai

1949 USN, weekly cargo flights Seattle-Adak, two years

MATS, weekly cargo fights California-Orient, one year

1950 USN, airlift and bush flying in Alaska, Petroleum No. 4 (PET 4) Project, two years

USAF, Korean airlift, 25-35 flights per month California-Tokyo, termination: February 1954

1951 U.S. Army, movement of domestic military personnel, 1951-1957

USN and Interior Department, scheduled passenger, cargo, and mail flights throughout the Trust Territories, 1951 to July 1960

MATS, en route service to military transport aircraft at Wake Island

1952 USN, modifications and overhaul of R5C-1 aircraft (U.S. Navy model designation of a C-46 aircraft)

1953 U.S. Army, 360 military dependents across the Pacific

U.S. Army, transportation of 3,400 military dependents Europe-United States, two months

1954 U.S. Army, transportation of 3,000 military dependents Europe-United States, January/February

Completed 43 months of Korean Airlift, flew 17,750,489 aircraft miles, 92,035 aircraft hours, 13.7 hours average daily aircraft utilization

U.S. Army, transportation of 306 military dependents Europe-United States, six months

USAF, miscellaneous flights, United States-Tokyo

MATS, 206 flights transporting 30,000 U.S. Army personnel and dependents across the Atlantic in a single month, believed a record for commercial airlines

1955 MATS contract to service and maintain all MATS aircraft in transit at Transocean's Wake Island base

1956 Established aircraft overhaul operation at Honolulu to aid Department of Defense. Contract, overhaul F-86 aircraft of Hawaii National Guard

1957 Awarded six months contract by MATS to fly 190 tons of cargo per month route support Travis Air Force Base-Japan

Taloa Academy of Aeronautics awarded contract by the 6th Army to train Army pilots for instrument ratings

1958 Operation Quick-Trans, one-year DC-4 cargo operation between USAF Bases in the U.S.

1959 AEMCO held one-year contract for supporting MATS trips out of Wake Island

Major Services on Behalf of Commercial Aviation

1946 California-Manila flight gave Philippines first postwar commercial air link with U.S. mainland

Contract with Philippine Air Lines to operate international service to the U.S. and Europe

Extended PAL California-Manila international service to Shanghai, re-establishing an important trade route to expedite recovery of the Philippines

Taloa Academy of Aeronautics established to meet GI and civilian need for airline pilot and air crew training

1947 Established operations and maintenance base at Windsor Locks, Connecticut, to supply Oakland base, and expanded exploratory and supplementary commercial operations to Atlantic and Europe

Made emergency flights from California to London and Paris transporting food and clothing to the needy of Europe

Transported 600 college students from the U.S. to Europe and return on foreign vacation trips, the first transatlantic aircoach service

Transported 800 deep sea fishermen from California and Washington, to Naknek, Alaska

1948 Transocean was the first airline to conceive of the idea and inaugurate California-Hawaii air tourist common carrier service. Later, other airlines and travel agencies also began booking group tours to the Hawaiian Islands

Pioneered mass air transportation of hundreds of thousands of pilgrims participating in the Moslem hajj traveling to Jeddah

Established operations and maintenance bases at Wake Island and Guam to handle its expanding commercial operations

Inaugurated twice weekly refugee service between Rome and Caracas, Venezuela

1949 Established division in the Middle East aimed to develop aviation in area

Contract to establish Pakistani domestic and international airline services for Pak-Air, Ltd.

Expanded commercial operations in Pacific and Atlantic to 2,134,644 revenue miles, 60,504,124 passenger miles, and 752,032 cargo ton miles—72 percent of total operations for the year

First TAL aircraft encircled the globe in March 1949. On board were Orvis Nelson and a crew of eleven. Aircraft left Oakland, proceeded to Bradley Field, Gander, Shannon, Frankfurt, Rome, Damascus, Syria, Karachi, Calcutta, Hong Kong, Okinawa, Tokyo, Guam, Wake, Honolulu, and back to TAL headquarters at Oakland. Total flying time: 94 hrs 55 min

1950 Start of the Korean Airlift. Commercial operations limited to meet travel emergencies. 35 to 40 monthly California-Japan flights, supplying 11 percent of the total lift provided by scheduled and irregular carriers combined

1951 Korean Airlift continued occupying most of TAL capacity

Inauguration of domestic service in Japan for Japan Air Lines under joint contract with JAL and Northwest Airlines

Carried 1,500 fishermen from California to Alaska

Entered into interline traffic exchange and ticketing agreements with major U.S. and foreign scheduled air carriers

Established Air Jordan—national carrier for the Hashemite Kingdom of Jordan

Initial stage of Trust Territory operation to provide scheduled air service to the Marshall, Marianas, and Caroline Islands of the Pacific under the auspices of the United Nations and the Department of Interior. Transocean continued to serve the people of Micronesia until 1960

1952 Korean Airlift continued. Commercial operations limited to special emergency flights

Later in year inaugurated U.S.-Europe cargo service under contract with Scandinavian Airlines System (SAS)

Modified and delivered a fleet of five DC-4 aircraft to Saudi Arabia, including one aircraft with a built-in throne for use of King Ibn Saud

1953 With declining military airlift needs, TAL again focused attention on commercial services

Inaugurated low-cost tour service U.S.-Hawaii

Contracted with government of Afghanistan to establish and operate commercial air service between Kabul and Cairo

Taloa Academy of Aeronautics trained twelve Japanese airmen for service on Japan's domestic airline

Contracted with Iranian government for management and operations of Iranian Air Lines

1954 Inaugurated international service, Tokyo-San Francisco for Japan Air Lines

Taloa Academy of Aeronautics expanded commercial training of airmen to meet demand of returning Korean War GI's. In six years the school trained 1,400 students from ten nations

Research division developed system of external aircraft warning lights to meet air transportation industry emergency

Trained and licensed pilots for Lufthansa, the German airline

Contracted with United Air Lines for major overhaul of DC-3 fleet, over 18 months

Designed and constructed DC-4 simulator for crew training, the first such safety device to be built by an airline

Thousands of monkeys carried from Manila and India to the U.S. in support of Anti-Polio Salk Vaccine Program

1955 Taloa Academy of Aeronautics introduced new training courses to train private and executive pilots for winter flying

Contract to supply navigators for Lufthansa's transatlantic service

1956 By its tenth birthday, Transocean had flown more than one billion passenger miles and eighty-five million cargo ton-miles

Taloa Academy of Aeronautics' DC-4 flight simulator used by MGM for the filming of scenes for *Julie*, starring Doris Day. The simulator was built by the company for its flight safety program and the cockpit interior was completely authentic

Renewed contract to provide airlift and mercy service in the nearly 3,000,000 square mile Trust Territory of the Pacific Islands, a service the company had rendered with distinction for the previous five years

August 1955 to August 1956, major overhaul successfully completed on twenty-one United Air Lines DC-3s

Performed major reconstruction on the Braathens airline DC-4s and performed major overhaul of DC-4s for Thai Airways

Inaugurated Honolulu and Pacific Islands flights as a supplemental carrier in accordance with a published schedule. (Transocean was the first airline to introduce the term supplemental, later adopted by the CAB which cynically spurned the very carrier that had generated the idea)

1957 Provided transatlantic services on the Hungarian Airlift and laid plans for tourist charter service to Europe

Established Orient tour program patterned after Honolulu tour operation

1958 Stratocruisers flew scheduled airline service Honolulu-Guam; also Oakland-Chicago/New York City/Los Angeles

1959 Stratocruisers flew scheduled airline service Oakland-Honolulu-Wake-Guam-Okinawa

1960 Transocean employees at Guam continued the Trust Territory operation until the end of the contract in July 1960

Flight Enterprises, Inc., continued operations on the East coast until approximately 1963

Aircraft Engineering and Maintenance Company continued operations under auspices of Atlas Corporation until 1964

Transocean Air Lines Facilities

OAKLAND General offices, hangars, maintenance, overhaul shop, ticket and traffic offices, 101,161 square feet

SEATTLE Offices, hangar and maintenance shops, 240,000 square feet

LOS ANGELES Offices and terminal space, 1,320 square feet

HONOLULU Offices, hangar, maintenance shops, ticket office, traffic office, dispatch office, 38,000 square feet

WAKE ISLAND Offices, maintenance shops, dining room, living accommodations and recreational facilities, approximately 81,000 square feet

GUAM Offices, maintenance shops, ticket, traffic and dispatch offices, and terminal building, 7,800 square feet

OKINAWA District sales and traffic office, 300 square feet

TOKYO Regional sales office and liason office for Japan Air Lines and Japan Maintenance Company contracts

NEW YORK Regional sales and traffic office

SOUTH CAROLINA Office and overhaul facility in Charleston

NEW JERSEY Office and overhaul facility at McGuire Air Force Base

In addition, offices were maintained at Gander, Shannon, Frankfurt, Geneva, Beirut, Amman, Teheran, Rome, San Diego, Panama City, Washington, D.C., Dayton, Teterboro, Jacksonville, London, Paris, Madrid, Copenhagen, Munich, Asmara, Dijbouti, Abadan, Kabul, Baghdad, Shanghai, Hong Kong, Manila, and Tel Aviv.

Transocean Air Lines Officials

BOARD OF DIRECTORS—1946
Orvis M. Nelson, Chairman
Ray T. Elsmore
Sidney J. Nelson
John McC. Hodgson
Warren D. Williams

OFFICERS—1946
Orvis M. Nelson, President
Ray T. Elsmore, Executive Vice President
W.E. Rhoades, Vice President
Douglass F. Johnson, Secretary
Sherwood A. Nichols, Assistant Secretary
George V. Nikolashin, Treasurer
L.G. Breitner, Comptroller

ORVIS M. NELSON
1907-1976
President

B.A. Franklin College, Franklin, Indiana, 1932; M.A., University of Washington, Seattle, Washington, 1944; U.S. Army Air Corps, 1927-1929, 1932-1935; graduate Air Corps Technical Training School, Chanute Field, Illinois, 1928; graduate Randolph & Kelly Fields, 1933; First Officer and Captain, United Air Lines, 1935-1946; Captain, United Air Lines, Alaskan & Pacific Operations, 1943-1945; Chairman, United Air Lines Pilots' Master Executive Council; member United Air Lines Pilots' System Board of Adjustment: First Vice President, Air Line Pilots' Association, 1942-1946; held CAA Airman's Certificate #29875, Air Line and Transport Pilot Rating, multi-engine aircraft; logged pilot flying in excess of 13,000 hours. President and general manager Transocean Air Lines, 1946-1690; Chairman of the Board, Aircraft Engineering and Maintenance Company, 1951; Chairman of the Board, Oakland Aircraft Engine Service, Inc., Director of Transocean Engineering Corporation.

RAY. T. ELSMORE
1891-1957
Executive Vice President

Colonel, U.S. Army Air Corps, Reserve; L.L.B., University of Utah, 1916; admitted to Bar, Utah, 1916; Deputy County Attorney, Salt Lake County, 1916-1917; U.S. Army Air Corps World War I, 1917-1919; piloted first air mail flight out of Salt Lake City, 1928, for National Park Airways, and flew as air mail pilot for National Park Airways and Western Air Express, 1938-1940; Commanding Officer 329th Observation Squadron, Air Corps Reserve Unit, for states of Utah, Idaho, Montana, Wyoming and Nevada for 13 years between 1919-1940; at time of Pearl Harbor, December 7, 1941, in command of 5th Airbase Group, Island of Mindanao, P.I.; supervised evacuation from Philippines of General MacArthur and his staff, and of President Quezon and members of his cabinet; left Philippines for Australia on night of April 29, 1942 on last aircraft leaving Philippines.

Colonel Elsmore was awarded the Legion of Merit for services on Island of Mindanao; on February 1, 1943, became Director of Transport, Allied Air Forces, Southwest Pacific Area, consisting of all U.S. Army Air Forces and Royal Australian Air Force Air Transport type airplanes in theatre when Directorate organized; awarded Distinguished Service Medal for his services in air transport; in October 1944, became Commanding Officer, 322nd Troop Carrier Wing operating air courier service for entire Southwest Pacific Area for General MacArthur's headquarters; held Army Command Pilot rating, with more than 15,000 hours of military and airline pilot time (by year 1949).

Colonel Elsmore joined Transocean Air Lines in 1946 as Vice President and one of the Transocean originals. He was appointed president of the airline's subsidiary company, Aircraft Engineering and Maintenance Company on June 2, 1948.

W.E. RHOADES
1906-
Vice President (Director)

United Air Lines pilot 1933-1942, Director of Transocean Air Lines and its subsidiary, Western Sky Industries, Inc., 1949-1962. Colonel, U.S. Air Force 1943-1946, Pilot for General Douglas MacArthur; awarded Air Medal Legion of Merit.

DOUGLASS F. JOHNSON
1913-
Secretary (Vice President/Director)

Graduate, University of California, Los Angeles, Economics and Business Administration, 1935; financial analyst with the State of California, Dept. of Finance, 1 year; junior member of consulting firm doing financial analysis and business administration, 3 years; U.S. Naval Reserve, 1931-1941, CAA Instructor in Navigation and meteorology, joined TWA as Assistant Supervisor of Navigation Training for ATC contract school, 1942; U.S. Navy, January 1, 1944, Lt. (jg); Flight Navigator for Naval Air Transport Service; Lt. Commander and Director of Staff of Admiral J.W. Reeves, Jr., Commander and Director, Naval Air Transport Committee problems. Sales Manager, Transocean Air Lines, 1946-1948; Vice President Sales and Director Transocean Air Lines, 1948-1950; Executive Vice President and Director of Aircraft Engineering and Maintenance Company, 1951.

SHERWOOD A. NICHOLS
1913-
Assistant Secretary (Vice President/Director)

Attended Midland Radio and Television School, one year; Station Attendant, United Air Lines, 1941-1942; Supervisor, Midland Army Radio Schools, 1942-1943; Flight Radio Operator, United Air Lines, 1943-1946; licenses, FCC Radio Telephone 1st Class, FCC Radio Telegraph 2nd Class; Chief Radio Operator for Transocean Air Lines, one year; more than 3,000 hours flying time (as of 1951); Executive Assistant, Transocean Air Lines, 1947-1950; Secretary, Transocean Air Lines, 1947-1951; Executive Vice President, Aircraft Engineering and Maintenance Company, 1950-1951; Treasurer of Transocean Engineering Corporation, 1951; Director of Transocean Air Lines, 1951.

During Transocean Air Lines' first year of operation the company was assisted by Paul E. Hoover, vice president of the Anglo-California National Bank of San Francisco, and Reginald S. Laughlin, San Francisco attorney and company counsel.

Other Members of the Board of Directors/Officers of Transocean Air Lines and Subsidiaries 1946-1960

SAMUEL L. WILSON
Executive Vice President/Board of Directors

JOHN M. HODGSON
Board of Directors

W.D. WILLIAMS
Board of Directors

J.A. ULLNER
Assistant Secretary

H. BRUCE OBERMILLER
Treasurer

RICHARD PETTIT
Executive Assistant/Legal Counsel

ALLAN A. BARRIE
Atlantic-European Manager, Taloa Trading Company

WILLIAM L. KEATING
Vice President, Operations

E.W. RINGO
Director of Operations, Atlantic-European Division (Vice President)

HARVEY ROGERS
Chief Pilot, Pacific Division

JOHN HOENNINGER
Director of Navigation

FRANK SOARES
Director of Communications

JOSEPH A. REILLY
Counsel, Washington, D.C.

ROBERT L. BAKER
Treasurer

JESSE H. BANNISTER
Assistant Treasurer

ROYAL MINSON
Assistant Secretary

ELIZABETH M. BERENS
Secretary-Treasurer

GLEN LEASON
Board of Directors

ONAT Originals—March 1946

Christopher Angelos
Martin Barstad
Arthur Bisset
Al Carvel
Edwin Brissey
Cyril Bunbury
Thomas Buckelew
Jerry Byrd
James Clarksen
Wayne Croyle
R.H. Elsmore
R.T. Elsmore
Don Gallego
A.B. Guinther
Roland Halper
James Helmer
Robert Judd
Francis Kennedy
Esther Lavagnini
Ralph Lewis
Louis Lombard
Daniel McCarthy
J.W. McCoy
Andrew McKelvie
John Markusen
Al Mays
O.M. Nelson
S.A. Nichols
Patricia Olesten
Russell Owens
Edward Ringo
W.R. Rivers
Charles Roach
Harvey Rogers
Floyd Russell
Arthur Ryan
Galvin Sargent
Thomas Sconce
Don Sheets
W. Simpton
Vivian Sims
Charles W. Smith
Frank Soares
Louis Sylvia
Claude Turner
Jack Ullner
Ted Vinson
W.A. Wakefield
Robert Walton
W.W. Warner
Samuel Wilson
William Word

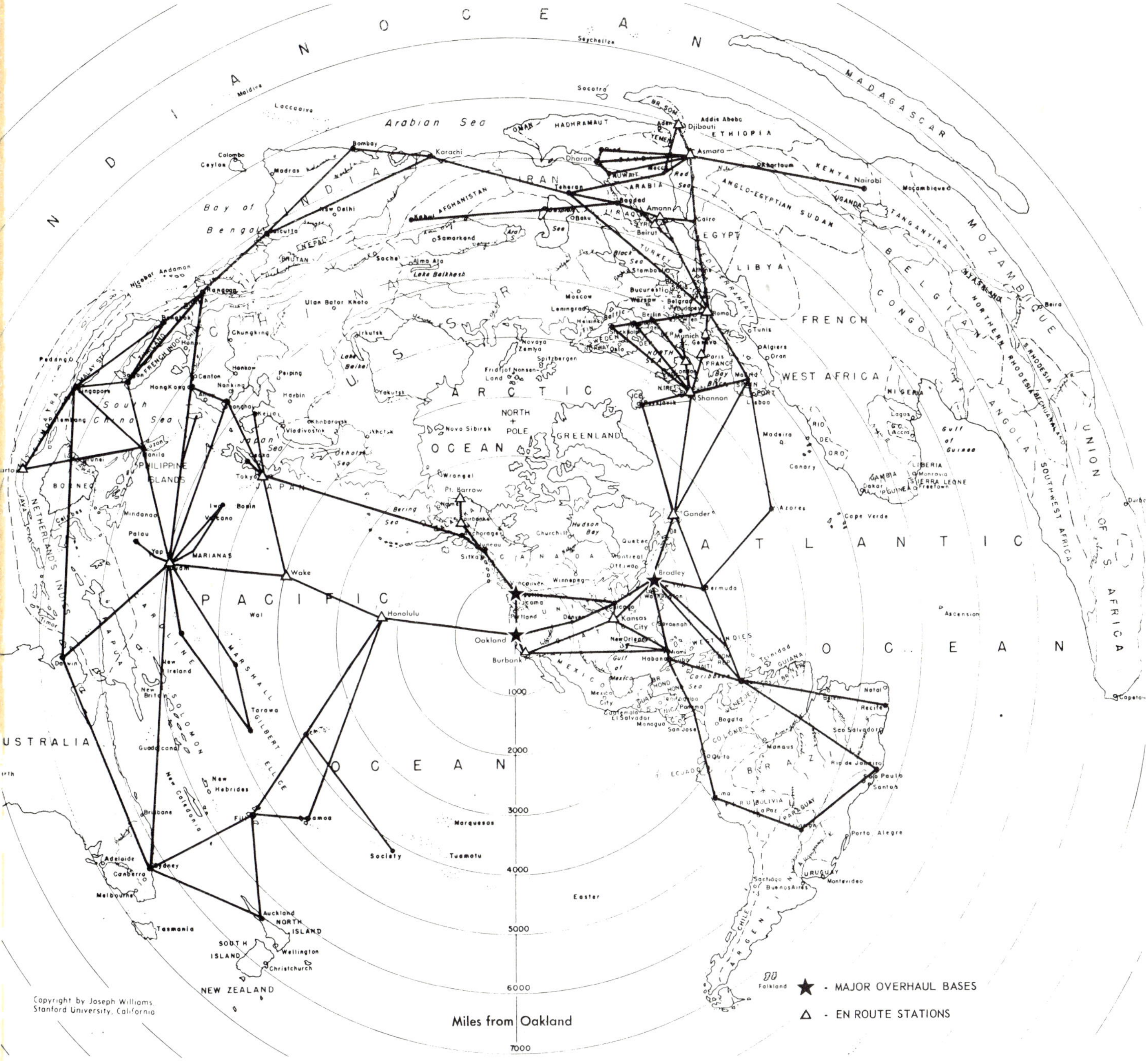

TRANSOCEAN AIR LINES

General Headquarters - Oakland Airport - Oakland, California - June, 1952

AIRCRAFT OPERATED BY TRANSOCEAN AIR LINES

MANUFACTURER	MODEL	REGISTRATION NUMBER	MISC. INFORMATION	PERIOD OPERATED
Boeing	Stratocruiser B-377*	N401Q		1958-1960
		N402Q		
		N403Q		
		N404Q		
		N405Q		
		N406Q		
		N409Q		
		N410Q		
		Total: 8		
	TB-17G	44-85607	LAES**	1947-1950
		Total: 1		
Cessna	T-50 (UC-78)	N2130		1948-
	170A	N3844V	TEC***	
	182	N5836B		
		Total: 3		
Consolidated	PBY-5A			
"Taloa Majuro"		N31232	Trust Territory	1949-1958
"Taloa Truk"		N31233	Trust Territory	
"Taloa Ponape"		N31234	Trust Territory	
"Taloa Saipan"		N31235	Trust Territory	
"Taloa Guam"		?	Trust Territory	
		Total: 5		
Convair	CV-240	N1018C		
		N1019C		
		Total: 2		
Curtiss	C-46E	N59487		
	C-46F	N4680V		
		N1300N	Mid-East	1949-1954
		N51424	Mid-East	1949-1954
		N51854	Alaska—leased from Golden North Airways	1950-1952
		N68963	Alaska—leased from USAF	1949-
		N68964	Alaska—leased from USAF	1949-
		N68965	Alaska—leased from USAF	
		N68966	Mid-East	1949-1954
		N68967	Alaska—leased from USAF	1950-1952
		N68968	Alaska—leased from USAF	1950-1952
		N68987	Mid-East/Alaska	1949-
		N74141	Leased from Pan American	
		N81954	Alaska—leased from Golden North Airways	1950-1952
		N92854		1958-
(Air Jordan JY-ABY)		N9900F		1955-
		Total: 16		
Douglas	DC-3	55L	Leased from Caralina Pacific Airlines	1958-1959
		2703A		
(EP-ACU Iranian AW, JY-AAB Air Jordan)		N33641	Mid-East	1954-
(EP-ADI, Iranian AW)		N3980C	Mid-East	1955-
	DC-3 B	N17314	Mid-East	1949-1954
		N54595	Mid-East	1949-1954
		N78907	Pt. Barrow Wheels-Skis	1950-1952

AIRCRAFT OPERATED BY TRANSOCEAN AIR LINES

MANUFACTURER	MODEL	REGISTRATION NUMBER	MISC. INFORMATION	PERIOD OPERATED
Douglas (continued)		N79907		
(TJ-ABH/JY-ABH Air Jordan)		N9896F	Mid-East	1949-1954
		Total: 9		
	DC-4	N1220V	Leased	1946-1959
		N226A		1948-
		N2750A	Leased from L.A. Air Service	
		N30042		1956-1959
(AW/EP-ADZ Iranian)		N30045		1956-1960
		N30048		1956-1957
		N30054		1956-1959
(JY-ABC Air Jordan)		N30069		1956-1958
		N4269		1956-1957
		N4664S		1952-1960
"African Queen"		N4665V		1953-1955
"Argentine Queen"		N4726V		1953-1955
		N4837V		1953-1955
		N4890V		1953-
(AP-ADK Pak-Air)		N48762		1947-1948
"Taloa Tokyo" (AP-ADL Pak-Air) (HZ-AAG Saudi Arabian)		N49288		1948-1952
		N50787		
		N5288N		1952-
		N54373	Leased from Seabound-Western	
		N57670	Leased from California Eastern Airlines	
		N60115	Leased from Pan American	
First Named "Miss Independence," then "Taloa Manila Bay"		N66635	TAL's 1st A/C	1946-
"Taloa Shanghai" (HZ-AAI Saudi Arabian)		N66644	TAL's 2nd A/C	1946-1952
		N67548		
		N68579	Leased from Air Carrier Service	7/1-7/23/57
(PI-C106 PAL)		N68923		
		N68942		
(HZ-AAH Saudi Arabian)		N68961	AED*****	1946-1950
		N68963	AED******	
		N68965	AED*****	
		N68967	AED*****	
"Kansas City Kitty"		N68969	AED*****(re-registered to N88796)	1953-
(YA-BAH Ariana Afghan)		N74648	AED*****	
		N75337	Leased from California-Eastern	7/3-9/2/57
		N75416	Leased from Trans-Caribbean	1956-
		N79000		1958-1959
		N79043		
(PAL)		N79047		
		N79048	TAL's 3rd A/C	1946-
		N79990	AED***** Leased from U.S. Overseas National	
		N79991	AED***** Leased from California Eastern	

AIRCRAFT OPERATED BY TRANSOCEAN AIR LINES

MANUFACTURER	MODEL	REGISTRATION NUMBER	MISC. INFORMATION	PERIOD OPERATED
		N79992	AED***** Leased from U.S. Overseas National	
"Taloa Calcutta"		N79993	AED***** Leased from USAF	
		N79994	Leased from U.S. Overseas National	
"Oklahoma City"		N79998		
		N79999	Leased from U.S. Overseas National	
		N88709	Leased from Northwest	
		N88756		1952-1957
"Royal Hawaiian"		N88784		
		N88785	Leased from Northwest	prior to 10/48
		N88817	Leased from Panagra or Northwest	
		N88818	Leased from Northwest	
		N88942	Leased from Pan American	
		N90405	AED*****	1948-1949
		N90407		
(HZ-AAF Saudi Arabian)		N90415		1948-1952
		N90427	AED*****	
(SAR-4 Saudi Arabian) (King Ibn Saud)		N90901		1948-1952
		N90911	Leased from USAF	
"Taloa Panama"		N90915		
		N95495	TAL's 4th A/C	1946-
(JY-ACD Air Jordan)		N9864F		1958-1959
		N9894F	Leased from US Navy	1955-1957
(Saudi Arabian)		N9937F		
		N9938F	Leased from Pan American	
		N9939F	Leased from USAF	1954-
(EP-ADJ Iranian AL)		N9940F		1956-1958
(EP-ADK Iranian AL)		N9941F		1954-
		Total: 68		

(Note: Some of the DC-4s were leased for short periods of time only. There were 14 DC-4s used in 10/47 for immigrant flights alone.)

	DC-6B			
"The Royal Hawaiian"		N90806	Pacific	1952-1953
		Total: 1		
Grumman	G-44 Widgeon	N68395	Alaska—leased from Jim McGoffin	1950-1952
		Total: 1		
	SA-16A	N9942F	Trust Territory	1958-1960
		N9943F	Trust Territory	1958-1960
		N9944F	Trust Territory	1958-1960
		?	Trust Territory	1958-1960
		Total: 4		
Lockheed	18 Lodestar	N54549	Executive Airplane, Oakland	
		Total: 1		
	L-749A	N9813F	AED*****	1958-1959
		N9816F		1958-1959
		N9830F		1958-1959
		Total: 3		

AIRCRAFT OPERATED BY TRANSOCEAN AIR LINES

MANUFACTURER	MODEL	REGISTRATION NUMBER	MISC. INFORMATION	PERIOD OPERATED
	L-1049G	N1880	Pacific	1958-1959
		N1927H		1958-1959
		Total: 2		
Martin	2-0-2	N93039	Japan	1951-
		N93041	Japan—leased to Japan Airlines	
		N93043	Japan—leased to Japan Airlines	
		N93046	Japan	
		N93048		
		N93049	Japan—leased to Japan Airlines	
		N93051		
		N93053	Japan	
		N93055	Airlift (MAC)****	
		N93056		
		N93059		
		N93060	Japan	
		N93061	Airlift (MAC)**** leased to Japan Airlines	
		Total: 13		
Noorduyn	Norseman	N49375	Alaska	1950-1952
		N75938	Alaska	1950-1952
		N61321	Alaska	1950-1952
		N55555	Alaska—leased from Ken Armstrong	1950-1952
		Total: 4		
Piper	Super Cub	N__661	Alaska	1950-1952
		1179A		1950-1952
		Total: 2		
Stinson	Reliant	N__051	Alaska	1950-1952
		Total: 1		
Travel Air	S-6000-B	N-9844	Alaska—leased from Archie Fergueson	1950-1952
		Total: 1		

TOTAL: 146 AIRCRAFT, OF WHICH 68 WERE DC-4s

In addition, Taloa Academy of Aeronautics had a total of 56 single-engined trainers at its peak

*Other B-377 Stratocruisers purchased by TAL but never flown: N407Q, N408Q, N411Q, N413Q, N414Q
**Landing Aids Experiment Station
***Transocean Engineering Corporation
****Military Airlift Command
*****Atlantic-European Division

Bibliography

BOOKS

Chronicle of the 20th Century, Chronicle Publications, Inc.

Costello, John, *The Pacific War*, Rawson, Wade Publishers, NY, 1981

Davies, R.E.G., *Rebels and Reformers of the Airways*, Smithsonian Institution Press, Washington, DC, 1987

Encyclopedia of World War II, Simon & Schuster, Edited by Thomas Parrish

Forden, Lesley N., *Glory Gamblers—The Story of The Dole Race*, Nottingham Press, Alameda, CA, 1986

Goerner, Fred, *The Search for Amelia Earhart*, Doubleday & Co., Garden City, NY, 1966

Goralski, *World War II Almanac 1931-1945*

Halliwell's Film Guide, Granada Publishing, Ltd., NY, 1980

Jablonski, Edward, and the Editors, *America in the Air War*, Time-Life Books, NY, 1982

Knight, Clayton, *Lifeline In The Sky—The Story of MATS*, William Morrow & Co., NY, 1957

Kurzman, Dan, *Day of the Bomb—Countdown to Hiroshima*, McGraw-Hill Book Co., NY, 1986

Malkin, Richard, *Boxcars in the Sky*, Import. Publications, NY, 1951

McGraw-Hill *Encyclopedia of Science and Technology*, 1987

Thruelson, Richard, *Transocean, The Story of an Unusual Airline*, Henry Holt and Co., NY, 1952, 1953

MAGAZINES

Elsmore, Ray T., "New Guinea's Mountain and Swampland Dwellers," *National Geographic Magazine*, December 1945

Esso Air World, July/August 1952

Esso Air World, Sept./Oct. 1955.

Mingos, Howard, "Transocean Air Lines," *Esso Air World*, March/April 1951

Thruelson, Richard, "The Daring Young Men of Transocean," *Saturday Evening Post*, Curtis Publishing Co., NY, 1952

OTHER PRINTED MATERIAL

Fairbanks Miner News, Fairbanks, Alaska

Statement by Orvis M. Nelson, President of Transocean Air Lines, Inc., Before the Senate Small Business Committee, Washington, DC, 1976

Addenda to Statement by Orvis M. Nelson, President of Transocean Air Lines, Inc., Before the Senate Small Business Committee, Washington, DC, by Edith Nelson, 1977

Annual Reports of Transocean Air Lines, and other TAL records, such as letters and publicity releases, as well as various newspaper and magazine articles about TAL by Howard Waldorf and other writers, plus interviews with many former employees of the airline

TRANSOCEAN AIRCRAFT ACCIDENTS

DATE	MODEL	REGISTRATION NUMBER	INFORMATION	CASUALTIES PASS.	CREW
1-27-48	DC-4	N79990	Door blew off in flight between Honolulu & Wake	0	0
8-15-49	DC-4	N79998	Ditched off Shannon, Ireland. Destroyed.	7	1
8-7-50	UC-64B	?	Icy Cape, Alaska. Destroyed	0	0
8-15-50	UC-64	?	Umiat, Alaska. Destroyed	0	0
3-12-51	C-46A	?	Umiat, Alaska. Destroyed	0	0
6-11-51	YC-74	?	Point Lay, Alaska. Destroyed	0	0
7-15-51	UC-64A	?	Umiat, Alaska. Destroyed	0	0
11-5-51	2-0-2	N93039	Tucumcari, NM. Destroyed.	1	0
12-30-51	C-46F	N68963	Fairbanks, Alaska. Destroyed	2	2
3-20-53	DC-4	N88942	Alvarado, CA. Destroyed	30	5
7-12-53	DC-6A	N90806	East of Wake Island. Destroyed	50	8
6-10-54	DC-4	?	Keflavik, Iceland. Taxi accident. Damaged	0	0
10-1-55	PBY-5A	(USN)	Ditched, Pacific Ocean, West of San Francisco. Salvaged	0	0
1-27-57	DC-4	?	Tokyo, Japan, Groundloop, Destroyed	0	0
			TOTAL	**90**	**16**

About the Author

Arue Beaulieu Szura is a native of South Carolina, but has lived in California since 1937. She is a writer who has published more than eighty articles in magazines and the Daily Review newspaper, Hayward, California. She also self-published three cookbooks.

The author worked as a secretary for Transocean Air Lines from March 1948 until August 1953, after which she served as secretary for Transocean Air Lines' Council #130 of the Air Line Pilots' Association until the demise of the airline in 1960.

She is a charter member of the Taloa Alumni Association, publishes the Taloa Newsletter, and is the unofficial historian for Transocean Air Lines. She is also a member of the Western Aerospace Museum, Oakland, California; and the International Women's Air and Space Museum, Centerville, Ohio.

Mrs. Szura lives in Castro Valley, California, with her husband, Mike. In addition to her interest in aviation, she enjoys traveling, reading, shopping at "flea markets" for collectibles, gardening, and making quilts for her four married children, eight grandchildren, and godson.

RALPH LEWIS PHOTO